NARCISSISM

A better way to understanding the disorder of narcissistic personality. Healing after emotional-psychological abuse. Building a healthy relationship after the end with your ex.

COVERT HARPER J.

Introduction

Chapter 1 Signs and Symptoms of the Narcissistic Personality Disorder and Their Traits

Chapter 2 Who Does the Narcissist Target?

Chapter 3 Narcissism In Real Life

Chapter 4 Developing Emotional Intelligence After Narcissistic Abuse

Chapter 5 Surviving Narcissistic Abuse

Chapter 6 Healing from Experience with a Narcissist   How to Defeat a Narcissist

Chapter 7 How to Get Over Them in Real Life

Chapter 8 Building Healthy Relationships

Conclusion

Introduction

What is Narcissistic Abuse?

Narcissistic abuse is any kind of abuse that is inflicted on a person by a narcissistic person. Unfortunately, many victims of narcissistic abuse are never aware that they have been abused. The only evidence that shows up in their life is the signs of the abuse. If a victim of narcissistic abuse does not realize the extent of the damage, they may eventually give up on life to the extent of committing suicide.

Narcissistic abuses vary in extent. Some narcissists are not violent but only use verbal abuses. Things get worse if a narcissist uses both verbal and violent waves of abuse. Narcissistic abuses target the mind, emotions, and the body. They will inflict physical, mental and emotional pain. The effects of any type of narcissistic abuse are far-reaching. The victims eventually suffer from Narcissistic Abuse Syndrome, PTSD, Anxiety or some mental disorder in their life. It becomes difficult for a person to have a normal life after experiencing narcissistic abuse. However, the extent of the damage also depends on the period under which the person was a captive.

Narcissistic abuse effects are usually far-reaching because torture is applied over time. Some individuals are held hostage by narcissists for decades. Being in the presence of a narcissist for such a long time eventually changes a person's perception of life to the fullest. Victims lose faith in humanity and lack trust in everyone. Even people who believed in love and trust, eventually lose their faith in such. Some victims go the extent of losing faith in God. If the torture goes on for a long time, victims usually result in suicide.

Understanding narcissistic abuses should help anyone in a narcissist relationship or family spot the red flags. Some of the narcissistic abuses may sound so innocent. However, when the abuses are inflicted on an individual over a long time, they take root. Narcissists target a person's values and beliefs. They inflict pain that eventually makes the victims feel worthless and lose their beliefs. If a person undergoes verbal abuse that gives them such an identity, he/she might end up believing the lies perpetuated by the abuser. Victims of narcissistic abuse lose self-esteem and self-worth. Once the abusive words get into a person's mind, the victim no longer sees a reason to live. They do not live because they want to but only to please the narcissist.

They give up on fighting for their dreams or anything they desire. A person who has undergone narcissistic abuse eventually agrees that the narcissist is better and superior.

Spotting narcissistic abuses should not be difficult if you have an idea of what narcissist does. They are all geared towards glorifying the narcissist while demeaning the victim. A narcissist uses words of abuse that directly kill a person's self-worth. They directly inflict pain using suggestions, actions, and words that humiliate and publicly shame the victims. Narcissists try to look good in the eye of the public and use their victims to do whatever they want. They work hard to hide their true identity by forcing, manipulating, and torturing their victims to do certain things.

One clear sign of narcissistic abuse is that the abuser does not have empathy. They may appear to show remorse later on but they surely enjoy inflicting pain. In most cases, they show satisfaction and fulfillment while inflicting the pain. They laugh, smile, and enjoy the suffering in of the victims all ways. When the victim is in pain and begging for mercy, the narcissist swims at the moment and glorifies his/ her personality. They do not show mercy or any feelings of empathy towards their victims. The first step to spotting narcissistic abuse is to identify the sociopathic characteristic of the abuse. Just like sociopaths, narcissists are dead on the inside.

They do not mind hurting or inflicting pain. The only difference between sociopaths and narcissists it's that sociopaths are not attached to the victim. Sociopaths can easily dump the victim and pic another to fulfill their desires. On the other hand, narcissists are attached to the victim for a long time, even for life. Narcissists will break up with someone for years and go back looking for the same person.

When a narcissist believes that someone is their gateway to something they want, they will keep on going back to their victim. They do not give up until they get that person to be a total slave. They use different types of manipulation, including seduction to get the person they want in the place they want,

Types of Narcissistic Abuse

Verbal Abuse

Verbal abuse is the most common type of abuse among narcissists. Before they get to violence, narcissists start being abusive to an individual verbally. They use words that affect the victim's emotions and mental capacity.

The characteristics of narcissistic verbal abuses include belittling, accusations, shaming, blaming, bullying, threatening, ordering, sarcasm, criticizing, undermining, opposing, blocking, interrupting, etc. However, such abuses can be inflicted by persons who are not narcissistic too. Anyone can inflict such abuses when angry. Before you label any of these verbal accusations narcissistic, consider the frequency of occurrence. You should also observe the emotions and reactions of the abuser during and after the abuse. Narcissists are not empathetic and draw satisfaction from abusing their victims. Even when they ask for forgiveness, they only do so to stop their victims from taking action.

Manipulation

Manipulation is another form of abuse that victims never realize. It occurs both during the early stages of friendship or relationship and also at advanced levels. During the early stages, manipulation occurs in the form of mental games. The narcissist uses trickery and pretention to get someone to do something. As the two parties get acquainted, the narcissist slowly starts putting on the true colors. After fixing the victim in a corner, the narcissist will use any form of manipulation to get their way. Manipulation is often expressed in the form of aggression or threats. A narcissist behaves like a wolf; he/she uses aggression to scare the victim into doing things. In most cases, the victim may do things that seem mutual but deep inside they are not happy about it. It is very difficult for many people to spot manipulation, especially those who might have experienced manipulation while growing up.

Emotional Blackmail

Emotional abuses have the furthest reaching effects on narcissistic abuse victims. Emotional scars may take decades to heal and in some cases, may never heal. A narcissist inflicts emotional pain knowing that it will break down the victim. Emotional abuses are aimed at making an individual feel worthless. They provoke the feelings of doubt and eventually introduce low self-esteem in the victim. Emotional abuses are characterized by intimidation, shaming, threats, anger, warnings, or punishment. A person who is under emotional blackmail experiences anxiety, fear, and obligation. Such individuals are afraid of making any decisions or moves. They are terrified by the thought of the narcissist spotting them. A person who is under emotional blackmail always believes that the narcissist is watching. Even when they are alone, victims are afraid of making any attempt at escape because they believe the narcissist is omnipresent. They believe that they cannot run away from the abuser and eventually resign to the fact that the life they live is the only option they have.

Gaslighting

Narcissists enjoy when they control a person to the fullest. They use gaslighting to get into the victim's mind and make the victim distrust their perception of reality. They use words to make you think that they control your life. They will make a victim believe that the reality is worthless. They make victims believe that they are mentally incompetent and unworthy of living a normal life.

Unfair Competition

Narcissists have a desire to show superiority, and to achieve that, they use unfair games. They will introduce all forms of competition in life. They may compete with the victim socially, academically, financially, or in any way possible. They introduce competition to show the victim that he/she is worthless and does not match the status of the narcissist.

Negative Contrasting

Narcissists constantly use abuses to compare their victims to other people. They unfairly compare them to previous relationship partners or friends. In a family setting, narcissists compare siblings against others. They use the victim's weaknesses to make them feel worthless and undeserving.

Sabotage

Sabotage is another form of abuse inflicted a narcissist. They often target anything that makes the victim happy. They sabotage any activity, achievement or objective that might make the victim happy. They may sabotage academic success, break up relationships or terminate the victim's employment. The target of a narcissist is to end up having the victim doubting his/her abilities. Sabotage of the activities and achievements are a prime target for a narcissist, especially when dealing with self-reliable individuals.

Exploitation and Objectification

When you are in a narcissistic relationship, you eventually feel like an object. Exploitation entails using someone to fulfill personal goals. Narcissists constantly turn their victims into tools and objects. They use their victims to achieve anything they want in life. Sometimes, they may go to the extent of using their victims to commit crimes such as robbery. Once they have a person under control, they might use that person to steal or rob or do any job.

Pathological Lying

Continuous pathological lies are part of narcissist's true characters. Although many people may not consider laying an abuse, it inflicts serious pain on the victims. They lie in relationships, finances, family and all matters concerning their life. The first step to discovering anyone's identity is demanding to know the truth. When a person is a pathological liar, they fail to say the truth about their family history, upbringing, or even their job. An inquiry to find out such factors at the early stages of a relationship might help save an individual from narcissistic abuse.

Withholding Privileges and Rights

Another technique used by narcissists is to withhold something they know that the victim needs desperately. They may withhold sexual intercourse, communication, or affection. In some instances, they go to the extent of withholding children's affection. A narcissistic partner may manipulate the children, making them withhold their love for the victim.

Neglect

Narcissists use neglect to make their victims feel useless and worthless. Neglect includes leaving the victim in an endangered situation. For instance, a narcissistic mother may leave their child without food or in a place that may lead to physical harm. Since narcissists are not empathetic, they are usually not moved even when their own child is in pain. The signs of neglect will show throughout their life. Narcissists may neglect parents, spouse, or children without feeling remorse or concern.

Privacy Invasion

A victim of a narcissist never has personal time. Narcissists abuse their victims by ensuring that they share every piece of private time. Narcissistic privacy abuse includes checking personal belongings such as wallets and phones, denying physical privacy even when the victim requests, following up or stalking the victim, etc. The narcissist ensures that he/she has every single piece of information about the victim. They follow every move that the victim takes and ensure that the victim does not make contact with anyone who might be of help.

Character Assassination

Narcissists thrive in making their victims look like the villains in the relationship. They spread rumors and accusations that eventually turn everyone against the victim. The victim is eventually painted as a public enemy, separated from family and friends and driven to a point where they do not have any support in life.

Physical Violence

Violence includes physical abuses to the victim. The physical abuses may get chronic and sometimes may even lead to murders. Narcissists try to use physical violence to dominate, bully and control the victims at any time. When a narcissistic relationship gets violent, it is at a critical stage and needs urgent intervention. In most cases, at such a stage, the victim is no longer in control. The victim might be already separated from friends and family. It takes courage or help of neighbors to rescue a person at this stage of a narcissistic relationship.

Violent abuses are characterized by pulling of hair, blocking movements, throwing things, destruction of property, kicks, and fists, bites, among others.

Financial Abuse

Financial abuses usually occur once the victim has been lured into the net. The narcissist gradually takes control of the assets and finances of the victim. The narcissist gains access to personal financial information, including bank accounts, credit cards, and investments. Once they are in the controlling seat, narcissists start controlling the victims' economy. The narcissist will use all types of dirty tricks to abuse the victim financially, including extortion, manipulation, theft, gambling, credit card theft, insurance fraud in the name of the victim among others. Narcissists who target victims for financial gains usually ensure that the take every single piece of wealth associated with their victim. They do not pay too much attention to the other person's feelings or state of life. They may leave the victim in huge debts and move onto the next victim.

Isolation

Narcissists enjoy inflicting pain and torture to victims after isolating them from family and friends. While they are in the process of isolation, it is not easy for an individual to recognize that they are being isolated. Isolation is an abuse since it causes emotional pain that may last forever. Isolation leads to broken families, friendships, and working relationships. Isolation puts the victim in a position of dilemma, leaving them with no one to turn to for emotional, mental or financial support. In this state, narcissists take full advantage of the victim, knowing that they do not have help from any other part of the world. In some instances, the narcissist may paint the victim in a negative light to break communication between the victim and family members. Eventually, it is the narcissist that paints himself as a good person and keeps on communicating with the victim's friends and family. The narcissist takes the position of a hero and makes the victim a villain such that no one can believe the victim even if he/she tried speaking out.

Sexual Abuse

In romantic relationships, narcissists thrive on sexual abuse. However, even in family relationships, sexual abuse exists. Children born to narcissistic parents may endure sexual abuse from a very tender age. Sexual abuse comes in many ways. It can be verbal or physical in nature. Sexual abuse my include touching, suggestive talk, demining sexual talk, ridicule of a person's sexuality, ridicule of the victim's appearance, weight or body shape among others. In most cases, victims of sexual abuse do not even know when being abused, especially in marriage. Sexual abuse in marriage may include being denied sexual intercourse, rape, the spread of sexually transmitted diseases, etc. A narcissist eventually turns their victim into a sexual object, which they use for self-satisfaction. The victim does not have a say in their sexual life and often has to oblige to the demands of the other partner. The victim is not allowed to request sexual intercourse but is expected to give intercourse on demand.

Sexual abuse happens to both male and female victims. Although male victims may not know when they are being abused, the fact of the matter is that forceful sexual relationship is equal abuse. These abuses may have far-reaching effects in the sexual lives of the victims for many years.

Chapter 1 - Signs and Symptoms of the Narcissistic Personality Disorder and Their Traits

How are the signs, symptoms, and traits of a narcissistic personality disorder recognized?

To be a happy person living a healthy, fulfilled life, it is normal to possess a sense of uniqueness and importance. Taking pride in our appearance and what we accomplish in our business or personal life is signs of a narcissistic personality disorder. It is normal to have these types of feelings about ourselves.

The difference between a person with NPD and those who are normal in their assessment of who they are is not that the non-NPD person does not view who they are as all-consuming and taken to the extreme. We don't obsess over who we are and how the world views us and how everything should be about us. We don't surround ourselves with status symbols or only associate with persons of prestige.

The narcissistic personality disorder is about a self-image that's distorted, unstable, intense emotions, and extreme concerns with adequacy, prestige, vanity, and power. Add into this mix an exaggerated sense of superiority and lack of empathy.

They talk about themselves continually – People with NPD think and talk about themselves continuously. They talk about their achievements, their appearance, accomplishments, or talents. Their achievements are always better than all others and they exaggerate about how attractive they are. Their comments are usually extreme and usually not a true reflection of who they really are.

They also lack empathy, never considering how others are feeling or asking others how they're feeling or about their thoughts. They don't understand or really care about the feelings and needs of others. You may have a serious medical condition and talk to a person about it and before you know it they've changed the subject and are talking about their recent vacation (George, Katherine, 2018).

They love to fantasize – according to researchers, people with NPD are apt to have minds that are filled with exaggerated and elaborate fantasies about their power, beauty, success, or their perfect relationships. They feel entitled to have the best of everything. All the status symbols like clothing, cars, their home, even brag about the schools they attended or places they've been.

No one as anything better than them, or are smarter, or more attractive. These fantasies fend off their emptiness, avoid their feelings of insignificance and imperfection. They feel special and in control and if they do not achieve what they envision, they can become extremely angry and frustrated.

They surround themselves with other people who they believe are like them, who are "special" by way of money, position or talent. These are the people with NPD want to be associated with.

The need to be praised constantly – Individuals with NPD give the appearance of being outwardly confident but their insecurity and delicate self-esteem have them craving for constant admiration and approval. They want to be recognized and feel the need to having people praise them even without accomplishing anything that actually warrants praise or recognition. Narcissists are also extremely sensitive to criticism of any kind. Any person or comment that highlights their deepest flaws or insecurities can be met with rage. The narcissist will divert the conversation into a different direction or just plain lie.

Their sense of entitlement – This characteristic is overwhelming. Narcissists have a sense of entitlement where they expect others to fulfill their requests and they feel they should get whatever they want with no questions asked. If they don't get what they want, they become angry and can even throw a tantrum much like a child.

People with NPD look at the world and feel it owes them. They look at other people and act as if they should be "serving" them and their needs. They act out when they don't get their way and their needs and demands are not met (George, Katherine, 2018).

Using others for their advantage – People are initially attracted to a narcissist because their personality exudes excitement and charisma and people initially find them attractive. Because of this attraction, people with NPD don't find it very difficult to have people do their bidding whenever they want it done.

Taking advantage of others when a narcissist's needs are not being met doesn't present a problem as far as they're concerned. They do it with little to no regard for the needs or feelings of others. Due to their un-empathetic behavior, narcissists usually have turbulent romantic relationships as well as friendships that are shore-lived.

Envy – A very common symptom of people with NPD is envy. They envy others for the slightest reasons. Their low self-esteem and need to have people see them as superior, narcissists see people who have things that they don't have as threats. It may be a car, more money than they have, position, even education, is the cause of envy by a person with NPD.

In order to combat their inner feelings of insecurity because of the perceived threat a person or thing may present, they tend to put it down with insults and acts to cause someone humiliation.

Individuals with NPD also believe that everyone is envious of them. Although they want to be envied, they will accuse those who they believe harbor those feelings about them and end the relationship (George, Katherine, 2018).

The center of attention – Narcissists LOVE being the center of attention. They need constant praise from their admirers to elevate and feed their low self-esteem. They feel superior to other people and desire attention all the time.

Narcissists feel compelled to talk about their exaggerated accomplishments and what they're doing or planning to do—they monopolize conversations, which are really monologues that's all about them.

There are two types of narcissism—vulnerable and grandiose. It is the narcissist who has the grandiose personality that desires all the attention and usually receives it by acting entitled, arrogant, and being outspoken.

Lack of empathy – Narcissists lack empathy. They do not have the ability to understand the perspective of others, cannot grasp the idea of their struggles and have the disinclination or inability to recognize the feelings and needs of others.

Narcissists can say something that is totally insensitive after having shown they could be reasonable. They could complain about how they're so annoyed about how their mother is to someone whose mother was just diagnosed with cancer.

The worst part of their insensitivity is that they don't believe they're being insensitive and offer no apology to those who may point out this flaw. If anything, the narcissist will become angry at having their flaw exposed.

They are insecure – People who suffer from NPD are extremely insecure which is the main reason they feel putting others down will inflate their ego and feed their sense of entitlement. The idea that a narcissist is insecure seems a strange thing to people who think they are charming and attractive.

The insecurity of a narcissist who is vulnerable comes from their questioning themselves whether or not they are really unique and special. They rely on affirmation from others to elevate their feelings of entitlement and greatness.

Narcissists have low self-esteem. Their drive is to prove themselves constantly. They don't just prove themselves to others as well as to themselves. This is afflicted fears and feelings of inferiority.

Their lack of self-esteem and insecurities have persons with NPD frequently "fish for compliments" from others by bragging and boasting about their achievements. In other words, they know very well how to compliment themselves while looking for compliments from others (Seltzer, 2013).

They can be defensive and self-righteous – Narcissists need an inordinate amount to protect their overblow but delicate egos. Their ever-attentive defense system is easily set off with little effort. For people with NPD, it's not only how they react to criticism but they react to ANYTHING done or said that they think is questioning their capabilities. This can activate their self-protective systems.

In their minds, people with NPD feel their survival is based on being justified and admitting they are wrong or have made a mistake and apologizing in extremely difficult for them.

React to opposing viewpoints with anger – Narcissists are not open to being exposed as "wrong" and express themselves with anger. Their anger is exhibited because they're feeling some humiliation or hurt that happened in their past and their anger is the consequence of these unwanted feelings.

They project traits and behaviors they themselves can't or don't accept in themselves – People with NPD are bound from deep within themselves to hide any weaknesses or flaws in their self-image. Because of this, they take any negative appraisal of themselves and redirect them on to others.

In other words, if a person with NPD is assessed as being wrong or bad or mean, their response is that "I'm not wrong (bad, mean); you are."

Their ambitions and goals – Normally, having an ambition or goal in your life is commendable but narcissists take their goals and ambitions to an extreme level. They're better than everyone, incredibly special, and set limitless ambitions and goals and fantasize about achieving more and better over all others.

Their fantasies are about how much wealthier and powerful they will become and how much better they will achieve their ambitions and goals than everyone else.

Their sense of superiority and entitlement is the reason that they will only socialize or speak to those they perceive have prestige and prominence. They will also fixate on status symbols, like the neighborhood they live in, the luxury car they drive, or the exclusive clubs they may belong to. They will deride and disparage those who they don't perceive to be on the same level or have the same kinds of "status symbols."

They can be charming – First impressions of beginning a relationship with a narcissist, whether a romantic one or one of friendship, begins with them being their most confident and charming, a pleasure to be around and get to know. However, it's the "get to know" part that's the tricky part because once you get to really know them, you most likely would like to "un-know" them. The relationships eventually develop where the narcissist's behavior becomes aggressive, selfish, demeaning, and irritable. They like to be in positions of leadership and love the power that goes with that position. Once they attain this position, they will manipulate others to do their bidding to get what they want. If they don't get what they want, they throw a tantrum.

If the teenager grows to adulthood and continues to build on their NPD characteristics, they continue to exhibit those symptoms.

Competitiveness is one of the common symptoms of narcissism. The person with NPD want to win at all costs, no matter what it takes. They are obsessed with winning and the person with a narcissistic personality disorder has no in between—there only winners and losers and they are not shy to point out others who they consider "losers" in order to elevate their superiority over someone else.

Their constant need to win negates any ability to praise or commend the success of someone else or are put into a vulnerable situation where they don't exhibit superiority over their opponent.

Grudges – The facade that narcissists exhibit as being extremely confident without a care of what others think about them is just that—a facade. In reality, they are sensitive to the extreme and really do care about upholding their "perfect, unflawed" image of themselves. They are not very happy when anyone insults them or shows their disapproval of the narcissist's behavior. They see these actions as "personal attacks" and hold spiteful grudges because of this.

The person with NPD will not let what they perceive as "attacks." If they feel slighted, they don't let it go or get over it.

They're not fans of criticism – For most of us, criticism is an acquired taste. We have had experiences where we've become frustrated over things turning out the way we didn't expect or was criticized and had a difficult time taking it from others. That is totally normal. We are only human.

However, the person with NPD to accept criticism and handle the idea they have flaws and are not perfect just doesn't happen. They are unable to cope with criticism and when things don't go their way will not admit they have any fault or they were wrong. Taking any form of criticism or constructive suggestions are impossible for them.

Narcissists react aggressively and defensively to failure or criticism. They cut the people off who are trying to be helpful and react with angry outbursts, yelling, or exhibiting aggressive behavior (George, Katherine, 2018).

One of the other aspects of their being reactive to criticism is that they feel it is inferred that they are being negatively evaluated for their performance or personality.

An example of this is being asked a question that they may not know or have the answer for which they feel is asked to expose a deficiency or vulnerability. If they can't answer they'll lie and change the subject or respond with an answer that has absolutely nothing with the question that was asked.

They have poor interpersonal relationships – Narcissists are not cognizant of where they end and others begin. In their minds, they regard other people as being in their "space" in order to serve their needs.

Narcissists put their needs first and regard other people as existing to cater to their personal needs without regard to the needs of those other people. This precludes that relationships with a narcissist usually ends because of a narcissist's lack of regard for others and lack of empathy.

People with narcissistic personality disorder have many shortcomings that they can't or won't recognize are harmful in their relationships with others. The underlying motivation for their behavior is insecurity which breeds the narcissist's fantasy of how great they are and their attitude of entitlement because of their elevated sense of self.

If these symptoms and signs are recognizable in yourself or others who you deal with, it may be time to rethink how it affects you.

Chapter 2 - Who Does the Narcissist Target?

The next topic that we need to take a look at is the type of person the narcissist targets. In reality, the narcissist can target anyone. Most people think that they are safe and that they are never going to be taken advantage of by the narcissist in their life. They think they are too smart enough or that they would be able to see the signs long before anything happened. But in reality, the narcissist is good at their tricks, and if they feel like they can benefit from targeting one person over another, it doesn't matter how smart you are or any other factor, the narcissist is going to do it.

It is important to always be on the lookout for the narcissist and what they may try to do against you. These people may give off subtle signs that they are about to trick us or cause some other issues, but we are too busy enjoying their tricks or assuming that we would never get caught that we don't pay attention. This is something that has to stop if you want to avoid some of the issues that come with having a narcissist in your life.

Now, we have just said that anyone can become a target of a narcissist, and this is certainly true. But there are certain groups of people and certain traits that the narcissist is going to look for when they pick out these targets. This helps the narcissist to find someone they can actually manipulate for their own needs and ensures that the narcissist is actually going to get what they want when it is all said and done. Some of the traits that the narcissist is likely to look for when picking their target includes:

You have something important that the narcissist wants.

This can be a whole bunch of things, including lifestyle, position, power, or money. When a narcissist is involved in any kind of relationship, the dynamic that shows up is going to be a bit different than what we would see with other relationships. It is going to start out with some kind of hook, one that makes you fall in love and helps you to feel that the relationship is all about you. But behind the scenes, the narcissist is pulling strings and making sure that they are the ones in control the whole time.

The narcissist is going to use any kind of trick that they can to get you to stick with them and work on the relationship. Sometimes, the narcissist is able to come across as someone who is helpful. But then when things are not working out the right way, the tables turn, and all of the blame is somehow on their target. When the target does catch on, or they try to get the narcissist to take on any responsibility or accountability for the bad situation, the narcissist refuses, and the tension is going to escalate.

You have a strong need to help out others.

What may seem like a really good trait to have, it can be used against you when a narcissist comes into the picture. They will see this caring and loving nature, and try to use it to their benefit. They know that you are going to step in and try to help them all of the time, even when they are mean and using you. And that guilt and shame for wanting to help more, and not being able to, is going just to make the situation worse.

At the beginning of the relationship, it is going to seem like you,and the narcissist are a match that was meant to be, but things are going to turn quickly. In the very first stages of the relationship, the kindness and the generosity of the caretaker is going to be expressed. The giver is going to have another person to dote on finally, and being the center of this caregiver's universe is going to be perfect for all of the selfish needs that the narcissist has at the time.

Yet, this is going to turn into an imbalance of power quickly. The relationship is slowly going to start adding in some intimacy to it, and the narcissist is going to bring out their full potential and power. They will try to absorb all of the resources, energy, and time out of the relationship will gaining more of the control to get what they want.

Your disposition is empathetic and compassionate.

While the narcissist is going to have trouble being empathetic to others around them, they do find that latching on to someone who is more empathetic is a great way for them to get the control and the attention that they want. Narcissists are going to have a reason for everything and anything that happens in their life, and they refuse to admit that anything is actually their fault. Of course, as their partner you want to be able to listen to them and help out, but when you catch yourself saying things like "I was just trying to be nice", and if you often feel like you are not really in a relationship, but more of a prop for the narcissist to use, then this is a good tip that you are in a relationship that is very unhealthy for you and that you are a target of the narcissist.

Even though empathetic people and personality types are often regarded as good, the narcissist looks for them in order to get more control and more of what they want. These personality types are more likely to feel sorry for others and to want to help out more, so they are going to be a prime candidate when it comes to working with a narcissist.

Your childhood happened in an environment that was dysfunctional.

Even your own childhood can work against you when you are dealing with a narcissist. Your past is sometimes going to make it hard to spot when violations of your boundaries happen, which can make it easier to ignore your instincts when you are dealing with a narcissist and when you feel like you just should not trust them.

You will quickly find that a narcissist is going to really dislike boundaries. This makes them stop and doesn't allow them to have the free reign that they want to cause the trouble they want. If they are able to find a target who struggles to set up these boundaries, someone who is not able to keep these boundaries, or someone who is willing to take on all of the blame when one of these boundaries is violated, then the narcissist is going to sense this and will use it completely to their advantage.

The narcissist wants to make sure they have a target who is going just to let go of the boundaries and allow the narcissist to do whatever they want. This allows the narcissist to be in control, and they can push and shove their way into any ending that works the best for them. If someone does have boundaries, the narcissist may spend some time trying to break these down and see how strong they are. When the target lets the boundaries fall, then the narcissist is going to hold onto them and not let go. But when the person refuses to bend or move the boundaries at all, the narcissist will eventually move on and find a more willing target to work with.

You feel lonely and a big need to find love now.

A motto that we need to remember when it comes to a narcissist is "Find a need, fill a need." Someone who has a lower amount of self-esteem is going to be a lot easier for the narcissist to control compared to someone who comes in with a really high sense of self-confidence. At first, the intensity that comes with the relationship the narcissist shares is going to be confused with passion, but we always have to remember that the narcissist is going to be incapable of transparency at all.

Over time, based on the analysis of the narcissist about when this should start, the intensity is going to wane and then a cold and calculating disposition is going to be left behind. This can leave the target wondering what went wrong with that relationship, and they will get desperate in order to find the person they thought loved them, the one they once knew. And this will be enough to keep them around even though the narcissist has no thoughts or wants to become that person again, and that love did not really love, just enough love bombing to keep the target under their control.

You often feel that you should take the blame for things, even if you didn't do the actions.

The narcissist is not able to handle any blame at all. Even if it is obvious that they were the ones who did something, and every fact and finger can point back to them, they are going to refuse to take that blame at all. This means that they need to find someone who is willing to take on that blame and handle the guilt as well. And if you are one of those people who have no problem taking on the blame, then this could make you a big target for a narcissist.

As the relationship with the narcissist starts to deteriorate more and more, the narcissist is then going to start to use blame and guilt in order to try and make their target feel like the problem. Individuals who are sensitive and empathetic are going to be very vulnerable when it comes to the blame game because of their reflective nature. The narcissist will use certain phrases and tactics, such as, "If you hadn't done __ or __, I would not have had to get too angry with you." By redirecting your attention over to what you did wrong, the narcissist will make sure that the attention is diverted away from them and the behavior they are doing that is unhealthy.

You try to avoid any confrontation and conflict.

If they are able to help it, the narcissist is going to try and avoid any confrontation and conflict that comes their way. They would rather sit back and have the attention and adoration showered on them, without having to defend themselves or fight with their targets at all. If they are able to find a target who doesn't seem to mind being quiet in order to avoid a fight, then they are going to be super happy about this.

Narcissists are often going to feed off of fear, and this helps them out because they can use that fear to create mirrors and smoke screens. Those who don't like to deal with confrontations are often going to be afraid of guilt, abandonment, and anything that could make them lose out on a relationship that they feel is important to them.

When a narcissist starts to react in a more violent way to them, they are going to trigger these kinds of fears in the target. And the target, in the hope of fighting off those fears and not losing their partner, is going to bend over backward in order to keep things as peaceful and calm as possible. Even though it may not make sense at the time, the more that you avoid conflict, the more attractive you will seem to a narcissist and the more they are going to view you as a potential target to use.

As you can see, there are a lot of different personality types that the narcissist is going to be happy to work with. If they feel that the person is going to behave in a certain manner that benefits them, then, of course, they are going to be more than happy to start up a relationship with this person in order to get more of what they want.

With this said, a narcissist is going to be the most interested in finding someone who is going to benefit them in some way. Even if you don't show a lot of strong characteristics that are listed above that the narcissist may like, they may still be interested in you if there is some other reason, such as prestige, success, and good looks, that they will benefit from. This is why everyone, regardless of their personality and who they are, needs to be on the lookout for the narcissist and some of the tactics that they are going to try to use against a potential target to get what they want.

Chapter 3 - Narcissism In Real Life

Friendship Situations

Jim Jones is one of the famous narcissists of all times. He was a cultic leader in the 1970s and his works have remained impactful in the minds of many up to date. He started a movement that was religious in nature where he acquired friends through enticement and manipulation. All the individuals who belonged to the inner circle thought of themselves as friends of the supreme leader. After some years, he brainwashed the minds of thousands, to the extent telling them that he was God. By the time he died, Jones had directly caused the death of over 1000 individuals, all of whom believed that they were on the right path. The schemes employed by Jones included befriending an individual, taking their wealth and controlling their lives.

This is the case with most friendships in narcissistic relationships. Friendship in narcissism starts by attracting the victim. Once you get into the box, the abuser starts using manipulation to gain whatever they want. In some cases, the abuser may be looking for money while in some instances; the abuser is only looking for friendship. You must understand that the narcissist can gain immensely from having a friendship with a socially respected person. If you are a person of high social standing and the narcissist tries associating with you, make sure you are careful. You should not be open to entertaining every type of relationship if you do not know the intent. When getting into friendships, make sure you do some background checks on the individuals. This is especially true when a new person seems to know you very well. Narcissists do a background check before coming in with their heart-melting gestures. They will do research about you and find out about everything you like. When they come, they can easily fit in your life by providing exactly what you want, or you are looking for from a friendship. Be wary of such individuals who seem to know exactly what you want and how you want it.

Family Situations

Narcissism can also manifest in families between parents and children. One of the most obvious cases is that of Joan Crawford, the renowned American Actress with her adopted daughter. For many years, Americans celebrated Joan for her screenplay prowess, but few could tell the truth behind the mask. Like all narcissists, she maintained a long perfect life in the public limelight while back at home things were going south. It was until years later that her daughter revealed the torture she had to go through growing up. As an adopted daughter she felt that she had been used as an object to glorify the actress. She laments about the actresses' insistent need for attention. She explains that the actress, would use any means possible to obtain attention from her including abuse. When she first published her book Mommy Dearest, it became an instant top seller, even being turned into one of the best movies about narcissism.

Those who are in the biggest danger of narcissism are children. In the case of Joan, her daughter was adopted when she was young and innocent. As a 10-year-old, she did not know how to differentiate between discipline and abuse. In most cases, she thought that her mother was just being a mother like all other mothers. While in reality, she was being abused. Children often do not know when they are being abused. And even if they know, they do not have the mental capacity to choose to step outside the relationship. Children who grow up in narcissistic relationships often end up being slaves to their parents for life. It is our duty to protect children from such abuses. Even though the child might not be yours, you must always be vigilant to see what a child is going through in your neighborhood. Constant voices of a crying child may indicate problems. Every child should have a normal life. If you realize that your neighbor's child never gets time to play or interact with others, he/she is overworked or is punished constantly, you need to take action. The child protection agencies are always ready to sweep in and salvage the situation. Keeping quiet may lead to a loss of life of a child.

Workplace Situations

One of the most obvious and open cases of narcissism at the workplace has been witnessed in the Donald Trump administration. As the president of the US, Donald Trump has publicly displayed his narcissistic tendencies including belittling others, boasting about his prowess and grabbing public attention. He is the most classical case of narcissism in real life and his office has proven it. Donald Trump is deemed to be controlling and as a result, he has failed to maintain a working relationship with most members of his executive. In 4 years alone, Donald Trump received over 10 resignations and dismissed over 20 individuals from office. Most of those who were dismissed have recorded statements that indicate that their boss is controlling, abusive, racist and sexist. There has also been a wave of accusations from women pertaining to sexual abuse from the US president.

Some of the famous names to part ways with Trump due to his superiority complex and controlling tendencies include John Kelly, former Whitehouse Chief of Staff, Katie Walsh, Whitehouse deputy chief of staff and Joe Haggin, deputy chief of staff (operations) among others. All these individuals have recounted scenarios where their boss was utter abusive, either verbally or suggestively. They all mention not having the freedom to do their work and always having to dance to the tune of the boss.

This is the most realistic situation that shows what a narcissistic abuse situation at the office looks like. If you are in a narcissistic relationship, you do not have the freedom to make your own choices. Everything you do is influenced by the narcissistic abuser. Donald Trump is one person who puts his thoughts and opinions above the constitution. When he wants something, he will use all means possible, including manipulation just to get it. A case in point, in early 2019, the president orchestrated the longest government shut down just to demand funds to build a border wall. He used intimidation and treated democratic members of congress just to attain his ambition.

Of you are in a working situation where you have to constantly do things to please your boss without following the law, you are probably under narcissistic capture. When you are held captive by a narcissist, everything you do is for them. You do not have the freedom to do anything that is pleasing to yourself. You must work hard to ensure that your abuser gets their demands. It is common for narcissists at work to take all the glory for success. Even if you are working in a group, the narcissist will steal the attention and claim all the glory for a successful project. However, if things go wrong with the project, the narcissist will shift the blame to someone else. Narcissists always believe that they are right. They cannot do anything wrong, and any mistake during the working process must be shifted to someone else. They often shift their mistake to someone they deem weak and powerless.

Relationships Situations

Narcissistic abuses in relationships always start off with simple verbal abuses. After creating an ideal relationship that may seem like a match made in heaven, the narcissist starts introducing complications one by one. One of the classical cases is that between RnB celebrities Rihanna and Chris Brown. In this case, the relationship looked like a match made in heaven. Chris Brown had managed to steal the public limelight and made the world to believe that he was the perfect man for the talented RnB singer. However, things started going south just some years into the relationship. Rihanna recounts instances of verbal abuse and sometimes physical abuse. She recounts being belittled by the singer and being told that she is not good enough. The whole case broke out one day when the musician took the abuse to the next level. Abusing her violently and leaving her in the streets.

Just like most narcissists, the singer later tried apologizing, with a sense of desperation. At the early stages of a relationship, narcissists are attached to the victims because of what they want. In this case, Chris Brown was attached to Rihanna because she is famous. He wanted to associate with the most beautiful and famous girl in the world. However, his sense of superiority took control. Soon as he got the girl to his side, he started showing tendencies of control and self-love. Narcissists quickly forget about their sweet gestures and start showing control and superiority once they get hold of the victim.

It is important to note that, narcissists may do anything to gain your forgiveness after an abuse. They will come to you and apologize desperately even crying tears if they think that you are valuable to them. They will use any means possible to have you back in their lives. However, if you prove to be stubborn, they will turn to manipulation. They thrive in manipulating victims and making them feel as if they do not have another option. Like in the case above, the best way to completely put a stop to narcissistic abuse is going public with it. Providing evidence that someone is abusive and shaming them publicly will stop that person from reaching you again. In the case above, Rihanna ensured that the abuser was put in prison and that he was restricted from being close to her. It is paramount that all the victims stay far away from the abuser. An abusive relationship may get even worse once the abuser gets access to the victim during an escape mission. The abuser often tries to instill fear by introducing more painful punishment to the victim. You must ensure that you are protected from the hands of the abuser by law and by close friends.

Chapter 4 - Developing Emotional Intelligence After Narcissistic Abuse

Once you survive a narcissistic relationship, nothing is more important than healing. You have to learn how to regain your self-esteem and control. Recovery is not just about getting out of an abusive situation; it is primarily about creating a new emotional safety net for yourself. It is possible that it might take you a while to get over your trauma, but it is not the end of the world. Recovery is a gradual but efficient process. The following are some of the important things that you must keep in mind when working your way back into normalcy:

- Self-soothing and grounding techniques

A narcissist will confuse your concept of abandonment. If you have had issues with abandonment before, they will get worse during your relationship with them. The betrayal and subsequent abandonment makes you afraid. You feel you are abandoned because you are not good enough. There are negative emotions that can emanate from this, including panic, depression and sadness. Many victims make the mistake of turning back to their abuser because they have learned to believe they cannot survive without them.

Grounding yourself can help you overcome these problems. It is normal to feel like you lack something in the aftermath of this abuse. However, you do not have to react or respond to it by going back. Your amygdala might attempt to hijack your emotions from time to time, and the only way out is to remind yourself why you are not going back.

- Ask for help

You might not be capable of handling your recovery on your own, so seek professional support. In the wake of a narcissistic relationship, you often feel you cannot trust anyone to understand what you have been through. The rest of the world feels alienated from you. Instead of seeing people as a source of support, you feel they will judge you and you hold back.

At the end of an abusive relationship there are so many things that are left unresolved. You have a lot of unanswered questions, unfulfilled promises, unreciprocated love and affection. All these are things that you might not be able to deal with on your own. It is wise to get professional help so that you can understand yourself better, and manage your expectations better too.

The pain you feel at the end of this relationship is two-fold. You are in pain because the one person you invested everything on has turned out to be the worst investment of your life so far. You are also in pain because the relationship that you had so much faith in did not work out. You, therefore, need to heal from these two situations to completely heal and move on with life.

• Stay away from your abuser

Resist the urge to reach out to your abuser. Even if you miss them, stay away from them. Cut them off your contact list and forget about them. The confusion you experience will pass. One of the biggest mistakes that many victims make is that even after they are done with the relationship, they still leave room in their lives just in case their narcissistic partner can come back. Forget about second chances. A lot of victims who go back to their abusers end up worse, and some end up dead. You don't have to reach out to them. Some narcissists will reach out to you after a long period of silence. They might reach out promising to change, telling you how things have been difficult in their lives since you left them. If you fall for this trick, you will never heal.

Whatever they do with their lives once you walk away is not your concern. They are adults and can make adult choices about their lives. You are an adult too, and your adult choice is to start afresh. The moment your abuser reaches out to you and you allow them a few minutes of your time, you are back to the very beginning. Never forget that narcissists always believe you need them more than they need you. They have a lot of tricks up their sleeve that will manipulate you back into their trap, if you allow them.

- Rebuilding your life

There are a lot of things that you can do to rebuild your life. Rebuilding your life is not just about reengaging people you had cut off, it is also about rebuilding your esteem and confidence. You have a lot of feelings bottled up inside. Don't keep them locked down, release them. Find different avenues where you can release your feelings.

Start writing, painting, gardening; or join a dancing class, an amateur sports team; and schedule social meetings with your close friends and have fun together. These are just a few things you can do to help you feel better again. Try and avoid risky or unhealthy behavior though, because these might end up in disaster.

- Accept your partner

You need to accept your partner for who they are. They are narcissists. They might be suffering from NPD. What acceptance does is to remind you that there is nothing you could have done to make them any different. They believe they are perfect the way they are. Since they cannot accept you as you are, it is best if you walk away and start afresh.

Accepting your partner's narcissism is another step towards forgiving yourself. You did all you could, but they could never change. There was never an intent to change in them. This will also help you overcome the feelings of self-doubt that you might have harbored for a long time.

- Forgiveness

Are you willing to forgive yourself for your role in the relationship? Forgiveness sets the tone for healing. Remember that forgiveness will only come after you have accepted your role in the relationship, and accepted responsibility for it. Everyone makes mistakes. It is normal to find yourself in a hardship situation out of your own doing. This is life, forgive yourself and move on. It is the things that you do and how you respond to these situations that will determine how your life turns out.

- Ease the pressure to recover

With your abuser out of the picture, there is a lot of pressure for you to recover and build a new life. Try to tone down the pressure. There is no time limit within which you must recover and start living a normal life. Your partner might have stolen your identity from you, but this does not mean you have to hurry to earn it back.

Recovery is a gradual process. Everything around you takes time. You have to readjust to a lot of things in life, and if you rush it, you might be overwhelmed. It is okay to feel sorry for yourself, but don't let it turn into self-pity, or you might turn into a self-loathing individual. There is no race to recovery, it is a process.

Fundamentals of recovery from narcissistic abuse

There are four important tenets that will define your recovery process, and help you survive a narcissist. Everything else you do throughout your emotional journey revolves around the following:

Self-esteem

Self-esteem is simply you supporting yourself. You take back control from your partner, control over your emotions, your behavior, actions, your mind and your body. Everything that your partner took from you is back in your hands.

Esteem is not just about yourself, it is also about the way you interact with the environment around you. It is about how you respond to people, institutions and so forth. It is important to get back control over your esteem, because without it, you will continue on the destructive path of self-sabotage that your abusive partner had led you to.

You have to learn to speak positively to yourself. Don't hold back from pursuing things that appeal to you. If you had resorted to substance abuse to numb the pain of your abusive relationship, talk to someone about quitting.

Having lived through a life where you were afraid to try anything, it is time for you to motivate yourself to throw your hat in the ring. You might not be selected, but you challenged for something. Take back control over your life.

Self-love

No one will ever love you more than you love yourself. Loving yourself is about protecting the things that are dear to you. Nurture your feelings and emotions. You have to stop sacrificing your needs so someone else can be happy. Make yourself a priority. Let go of the tendency to abandon your needs for the sake of a superficial connection with someone else.

One of the ways you can go about rekindling your self-love is to realize the things that you can control in life and those that you cannot. Remind yourself why you feel it is necessary for you to change something in your life. For most ladies, one of the things they have to deal with is body shaming when they get out of a narcissistic relationship. You have to learn to accept and appreciate your body the way it is.

In case you are worried about things that you are unable to change, teach yourself to drown those emotions and sentiments instead. Find things that you are grateful for and enjoy doing them. If possible, do them with people who are close to you so that you remember just how amazing your life should be, and embrace it.

Self-trust

Fear and doubt are common in victims of narcissistic abuse. Your partner made sure the only person who made decisions in your life was them. They took away your ability to decide what you want or how you want things done. They became the ultimate source of power in your life.

When you are unable to trust in yourself, you struggle to do things. You cannot make quick decisions because you are afraid you might choose the wrong thing. Your worry is that all the bad things you have experienced might happen to you if you decide for yourself. As a result, you second-guess yourself all the time.

Trust in your gut. Do something because you feel it is right. Don't hold back. To rebuild trust in yourself, you must take action. It is impossible to do this without stepping out and challenging yourself to try.

Self-worth

Why is it important that you rediscover your self-worth after walking away from a narcissistic partner? Self-worth is about realizing what your value is. When you understand your worth, it is difficult for someone to begrudge you what you deserve. Your value system sets you up high, and people who interact with you do so because they understand and appreciate how you treasure yourself. If you can't see your worth, no one else will. Even those who do will never take you seriously.

The challenge with lacking self-worth is that you usually end up compromising where you should not. Lack of self-worth also makes you feel ashamed and unworthy even without anyone provoking a reaction from you. You inherently believe you don't deserve the good things because you are not good enough.

Speak up for your rights. Don't shy away from the spotlight. Someone might use this to take advantage of you. Respect and take care of yourself. To rebuild your self-worth, you must embrace courage. You have to realize that even if things get difficult, you will make it.

Resetting boundaries after surviving a narcissist

Emotional abuse in a relationship usually comes with breached boundaries. You love a partner who doesn't recognize your need for or respect your space. People view boundaries in different ways. Their reaction to you having boundaries in the first place might not always be what you expect.

Some people react negatively, and others even turn cold towards you when you mention your boundaries. Should you back down? No, not at all. Boundaries are the essence of who you are. They are a representation of your thoughts, feelings and what sets them apart from everyone else. Boundaries are your ethical code, they determine wrong from right and give your life direction.

With boundaries, you can protect yourself from exploitation and manipulation. You also have limits to the things you can do for people. A narcissistic partner will usually break your boundaries. They don't respect you and this makes you feel unnecessarily vulnerable. At the end of that relationship, you should find a way to reestablish your boundaries.

The good thing about rebuilding your boundaries is that you also rebuild your esteem in the process, and as time goes by, you learn to love yourself again. You learn to trust and believe in yourself. How can you reset and rebuild your boundaries after such a traumatic experience?

•   Rethink your values

Your core values are the foundation of your boundaries. Take time and re-examine them afresh. These are the principles and guidelines that control your life. They are the things you hold in high regard, like respect, honesty, affection, humility and loyalty. It is important to understand your values because they help you make the right decision.

A decision system should always be based on the things that align with your core beliefs. By understanding your values, you are in a better position to understand how to react or respond to different situations. You know what to do when facing a difficult situation. You know why it is important for you to walk away from someone because they don't fit in with your values.

These are decisions that do not just protect you, they also help you live a life you are proud of and you are at peace with your decisions. This way, you cannot second-guess yourself. If you have to make a big decision, you do so because you know it was the right thing to do. If it turns out wrong, you don't feel bad about it because you know it was still the right decision for you.

- Learn to say NO!

A narcissist will make you learn how to feel guilty each time you don't respond to their needs the way they want you to. Being a yes man or yes woman is exhausting. You never do anything for yourself. You never think for yourself. Your life revolves around what other people think or what they want you to do. Learning to say no is not just about stopping someone from exploiting you, it is also about respecting yourself. It takes nothing from your humanity or personality to say no. Don't fall for the trick when someone tries to guilt you into believing saying no will appear aggressive or pushy. A subtle no is all you need, and stand by it. To protect your boundaries, you must learn to be selfish. Your integrity is tested each time someone tries to have you go back on your no. Another problem you must overcome is the need to explain your reasons. A simple explanation is sufficient. However, if you over-explain yourself, this is a sign that you worry about what people think about you. It is a sign that you need to stop pleasing people all the time and be bold in your decisions.

At times, you don't necessarily need to explain your no. It might be a new experience for you, but give it time. It will grow on you. Some months or years down the line, you will realize it was one of the best decisions you ever made.

- Responsibility to yourself

Your responsibility in this life is to yourself. A life without boundaries opens you up to accept all manner of rubbish from your abuser and anyone else who can take advantage of you. You meet emotional wrecks who feel you can nurture them back to the person they are supposed to be. However, while you take care of them, they chip away at your personality and stability gradually.

You cannot be responsible for someone else's emotional wellbeing. If you allow them in, they will drain you. Why should you be exhausted from dealing with someone's trauma, and as they go away feeling happy and relaxed, your life falls apart because you can barely breathe?

While the emotional challenges you have experienced over the past might make you think you must take care of someone else's feelings, this is not true. Most narcissists simply project their baggage onto you and make you carry their weight alongside yours. You can understand them, but you cannot process the meaning and value of their emotions on their behalf. Step aside and let everyone deal with their own baggage.

- Respect your boundaries

There would be no point in setting boundaries if you were not going to follow through. Granted, this might be a new process for you, but it does not mean you will not hack it. For someone who has never had boundaries in their life, you must learn where to draw the line. You must be the first one to respect your boundaries before you expect someone else to do the same.

If this is your first time setting boundaries, start with simple things and learn to respect them. From there, build on to deeper stuff like your emotions. The discomfort you feel when rejecting someone because they don't respect your boundaries is normal. You are protecting something bigger than their feelings. Besides, they are responsible for their feelings. You are responsible for yours and your happiness.

To respect your boundaries and make them stick, you must be assertive in the approach you use. Don't bend the rules for anyone. This only makes you weak, and after a while, you will not respect your boundaries either. Everything that happens after you walk away from a narcissistic relationship is to help you become better. You are now in full control of your life, and you can steer it in whichever direction you please.

Chapter 5 - Surviving Narcissistic Abuse

No matter how a relationship of this nature has put you down or worn you out, you can rise again. Despite the abuse and strife, all the mind games, you can come out strong and regain your sanity. Narcissism exists in different phases of life relationship. It is not only peculiar to romantic relationship; narcissism exists in business and work, among families, siblings, and friends. But before we explore that, we should talk about the psychological effects narcissism has on victims.

Impact of Narcissism on the Brain

Many people find themselves stuck in abusive relationships. It could be emotionally abusive parents or people in a narcissistic relationship. The effect is almost the same which is more than mere emotional and physiological damage.

Neuroscientists have revealed that narcissistic abuse can cause physical brain damage in victims.

When exposed to emotional trauma for an extended period, it can trigger symptoms of PTSD. This is why the remedy for abusive relationship is to leave. Walk away before you lose your entire self to this person. Unknown to many, the long-term effect of narcissism is way more than emotional and psychological distress. What many do not know is that the brain is actually damaged by regular exposure to emotional abuse. With this prolonged exposure to abuse, the amygdala can swell and some experience a reduction in the size of the hippocampus (Morey, 2012.) The after effect of this is horrible but to understand why, we must understand the role of the amygdala and hippocampus.

The amygdala is responsible for negative emotions such as fear, anxiety, worry, guilt, and shame. The hippocampus helps in the formation of memories as well as learning.

To effectively learn as humans, we should be able to retain information into short term memory. This is the first step to learning. This needs to happen before any information gets transferred to long term memory. In other words, short term memory is as crucial to learning as long term memory.

Damage to the hippocampus produces a devastating effect. According to a study at the University of New Orleans and Stanford University, it's been discovered that a reduction in hippocampus is linked to high levels of cortisol (a stress hormone) in the body (Carrion, 2007.) In other words, excess stress in people makes the hippocampus smaller.

The amygdala, known as the reptilian brain, is in charge of emotions such as fear, hate, lust, etc. This is also related to breathing and heart rate. It is responsible for triggering the fight and flight response.

Victims of narcissistic abuse are always in a state where their amygdala is on high alert. With time, these people transition to a state where fear and anxiety becomes a constant, and the amygdala will pick up on the slightest sign of abuse.

Even after the victim has left the abusive relationship, there are lingering signs of post-traumatic stress such as panic attacks and excessive phobias. This is because the amygdalas increased size now considers the state of fear and anxiety as normal. To try and keep themselves from the reality of the situation, the victims use reality twisting devices such as:

Projection: In a bid to try and deny the facts, victims choose to believe that the narcissist is not all that bad. They want to believe deep down there is compassion. This most of the time is a lie.

Denial: Victims refuse to accept the gravity of their situation. They convince themselves that living with it is better than confrontation.

Compartmentalization: Victims ignore the abusive aspects of the relationship and choose to focus only on the positive ones.

Gradual Damage of the Hippocampus

The right function of the hippocampus helps us read, study, understand, and process information. In other words, the hippocampus handles everything that relates to learning and knowledge. Since it relates to learning, it is associated with the formation of new memories. This crucial part of the brain is negatively affected by stress due to the presence of cortisol. Cortisol decreases the size of the hippocampus when it fights the neurons. This makes us more subjected to stress and anxiety. The more these distressing emotions thrive in the brain, the more our brain is changed.

Stress from narcissistic abuse, both short terms, and long-term stress duration are equally damaging. As a result, even subtle abuse and manipulation from the abuser can destroy the victim's brain.

The good news, however, is that you can take helpful steps to heal your brain and get it back to normal. Research shows that with methods like Eye Movement Desensitization and Reprocessing therapy, victims who have PTSD can grow 6% of the hippocampus in only a couple of sessions.

With many methods of healing available to those who experience abuse, you can reconfigure the brain to have a normal reaction to stress.

Surviving Narcissistic Abuse in Families

Do either of these scenarios sound familiar?

· A mother who tells her daughter no man will want her if she is fat

· A father who lies to his children and dismisses their opinions, all to get them to do things for him

Some levels of narcissism are prevalent in most families. There are many tactics a narcissist's parent could choose to exert on their children. This often has a profound effect on the child creating deep and painful wounds on the child's mental state. Being raised by a narcissistic parent can be devastating and potentially degenerating, causing low self-esteem if left unaddressed by the adult.

Naturally, it is believed that love should be instilled in all parents. There should be this unbroken bond that connects parents to their children. Looking specifically at the kind of intimacy a child shares with the mother, you expect to find an unbreakable chord of love that brings them together. However, not every mother is capable of unconditional love.

Some parents have been so eaten away by their past traumas that they don't see their children as a special human being deserving of their love. Instead, these parents only see them as an extension of themselves. This explains why they perceive their children as competition, a source of jealousy, and sometimes even a threat. To the narcissist parents, the youngsters are objects hindering other personal needs.

Being raised by a narcissistic parent can be devastating for a child. However, healing is possible as soon as they realize it's important. Now you don't need to spend a lifetime trying to mend your broken and damaged self-esteem due to your parents. To heal, you have to keep these thoughts in mind:

· Mourn: You were robbed of a normal childhood every kid deserves. Remember this and mourn properly as you would when losing something important.

· Accept: You see another child's mother and wish yours was like that. You need to accept that your life is just different from others, and that's OK.

Your upbringing has little to do with you, it was just an unfortunate turn to be born into a broken home, devoid of love and normal human emotions. You need to accept that this is who your parents were, and make the best of it.

This process of grieving and accepting is primal to healing. This is not about healing the relationship with your parents, but the relationship with yourself. Continuous exposure to abuse or neglect from your parents may have eroded your self-esteem, lowered your confidence or made you feel unworthy of love but there's always a chance to improve. The love, care, and attention that you never received from your parents can instead come from you. Other healing techniques are:

Get Rid of Your Inner Critic

During the abuse while with your parents, you believed that they might love and accept you if you were more talented or smarter. When this never happened, you resolved that you were clearly unlovable.

This left the voices of your parents in your head always criticizing and being negative. Allowing behavior like this to continue will only start a cycle of shame and abuse. Be kind to yourself and understand that no one is perfect.

Embrace Your Inner Child

You may think blocking it out is the way to cope. Nope. Think deeply about your feelings at this time. Look inward, and see yourself when you were criticized and felt unloved. Embrace this helpless child and develop a strong, safe, loving relationship with that person, it is you after all. Rather than constantly criticizing yourself, try to see the flaws in a different way. With warmth and acceptance, embrace this poor damaged kid with compassion.

Exercise Self-Care

Living and growing up with narcissistic parents might have conditioned your way to not focus on your needs. You only seek to please them and do what you think makes them happy. As a result of this, you are completely lost on how to embrace your needs.

Fix this by treating yourself. Do something just for you, spend time alone to really begin to love for yourself, maybe an activity or adventure that makes you nothing but happy. You and your needs matter.

Considering a child spends an average of fifteen years living under the pressure of a parent, with narcissists that time might feel like an eternity. Abuse doesn't happen overnight, or over the span of a year, so the journey to recovery can be long and at times hard.

Good things take time, allow yourself to take the time you need while being surrounded by people you love. In time, you will see visible improvements in every aspect of life, developing a healthy and loving relationship with yourself and others are just the baby steps you need to begin.

Healing Narcissistic Abuse in Relationships

Suffering mental, physical, and emotional abuse at the hands of a narcissist can be one of the most challenging things to get through. It affects every part of the victim's life, eroding their confidence and making them doubt themselves. Constant attacks with no relief or time for the mind and body to process the attack, let alone heal is why many people end up with symptoms of PTSD.

The following steps can help the healing begin:

Have Ironclad Boundaries

To heal yourself from an abusive relationship, you need an imaginary barricade to keep the negativity out, in the form of boundaries. This is the foundation for your healing journey to get off the ground. Thinking you're out of the fray leaves you vulnerable to the narcissist, potentially giving them another chance to mess with your head. This contact can trigger pain that can pose as a major setback.

While the best method is to physically stay away from them, you can also give them the cold shoulder, or just ignore them as stated before if getting away isn't easy. Leave no opportunity for them to prey on your emotions. Be emotionally distant even while interacting with them.

You also need to learn object. This is a gradual way to build your self-esteem and regain your confidence.

Forgive Yourself

Some part of you knew something was not right, but you were so drunk in love you didn't realize. This can make you shoulder the blame and be too hard on yourself. This won't help. Anybody could have been the victim, you were just in the right position to get in bed with a broken person.

You were manipulated, tricked, and brainwashed. You could not have seen it coming even if there were a ton of warning signs. Realize that you are a whole person, full of love and deserving of love. You are kind, smart, and worthy. It is the narcissist's loss for not knowing your true worth.

Adjust Your Focus

Having spent a lot of time with your abuser, there will an overload of moments to reflect on. This is a trauma bond–a sign that there are unprocessed emotions you need to deal with. The idea here is to find time to work on this with mindful intention, rather than being dragged by your past forever. Embrace mindfulness and engage in visualizations of a bright and hopeful future.

The narcissist may have made you bench your dreams for theirs but it's time for you to start working on them again. With a revitalized sense of purpose, you can get rid of the lingering thoughts of abuse that will hold you back.

Release the Abuser

The relationship with an abuser, often, is filled with anxiety and fear. You walk on eggshells anxious that the next thing you want to do will trigger their rage, causing a fight and a further unpleasant situation. There is a tendency for this to continue, long after separation from the narcissist.

While we do not doubt the fact that narcissists love losing and could be stubborn in their pursuit, realize that they are not as strong as you think. They only want you to believe they are.

With this in mind, the ability to get rid of the trauma hook bond will help you disarm them. You can now become established and resolute. Unwavering even in the face of all their issues and drama.

Practice Mindfulness

When you stay long in an abusive relationship, you subconsciously transport yourself into a state of hyper-vigilance. You are always careful of your moves, afraid of doing anything to spook your abuser. This creates excessive stimulation of the sympathetic system, which leads to an influx of adrenaline and other stress chemicals into the blood.

The key to deactivate this is to activate the parasympathetic system. In other words, you are transitioning from fight or flight mode to rest mode. This comes from various methods such as deep breathing, mindfulness, or any activity that relaxes and eases your anxiety.

All in all, know that you can heal and break free from the shackles of an abusive relationship. Your effort to heal and recover yourself can be a ticket to a whole, integrated, and complete human being. You can improve!

Narcissism Among Friends

Friendship is a beautiful gift. You choose those that surround you, these friends help make the world seem a little brighter and life worth living. Friends are there to hold and catch us when we fall and the people we are close to receive the investment of our trust and emotions. This bond can be overlooked by many, taking it for granted.

However, there are some instances where disturbing patterns, pain, and an unhealthy attachment that seem to characterize a friendship. Some people are trapped in a narcissistic friendship without any idea what that means, just that they are unhappy. Believing in someone's goodness is the basic symptom of humanity. You hang on for the ride, longing for the friend you once knew to come back. Unfortunately, there are times when things can never go back.

Holding on too long can open you up to narcissistic abuse. Due to the attachment, our narcissist friend finds it easy to prey and impose on us. They see us as an extension of themselves, and nothing we ever do is good or acceptable. Worst of all, you never seem to agree on anything as your narcissist friend believes their opinion is more important, and right.

Rather than enjoying the benefit that comes from having a friend, the benefits of the relationship are one-sided. You are there to meet their needs and soothe their ego. Saying sorry is not in their dictionary, and they will never accept that they have done anything wrong.

Holding on to this friendship for long starts taking its toll. By desperately trying to fix our broken friendship, we drown. Our self-worth, self-esteem and self-confidence then suffer for it. The relationship becomes draining and you are exhausted, trying to salvage it. Narcissism is real and plagues every facet of human relationships. Even though it is a lot to take in, many people find themselves in this kind of relationship. It is disappointing and shocking that such a thing could occur among friends, but that is the reality.

If you have found yourself in this kind of relationship, here are some tips to keep your sanity intact:

Be Good to Yourself: You do not need another person to complete you. Any friend that takes advantage of you should be cut out of your life. Realize that friendship does not add value to you and is not worth the time.

Free Yourself: While there is nothing wrong with trying to help your friend, just know when to draw the line. This might be difficult because letting go of a friend isn't always easy. But what friendship is worth the exhaustion?

Know What You Will Tolerate: Narcissists, even in friendship, sees everyone as less than themselves. In their world, they are superior, so they expect to be treated like it. They also operate with the mindset that they can treat everyone like trash and a nobody. Know your self-worth, and what you will not tolerate from your friend. Know when to draw the line.

Know When to Get Help: being in a narcissistic relationship is complicated and draining. It takes its toll on almost all areas of life. There are times you might need to seek outside help in order to recover from the anguish of dealing with a narcissist. There are support groups and therapy that can be of help.

Knowing when to walk away from a friend, or relationship takes courage. It can be a lot to process, which hurts. However, you need to protect yourself from a friendship that drains the life out of you.

Workplace Narcissism

Narcissists are peculiar people, they are easy to spot from an outsider's perspective. They occur in every facet of human interactions, that includes the workplace. They are typically obnoxious, overly outspoken and can make everyone around them uncomfortable.

Using various manipulation techniques like mind control, they find it easy to get people entangled in their web. As master manipulators they can put up a front to get on the good side of people. They are charismatic, the life of the party, risk-takers and they know how to get others to do things for them. This makes it easy for them to rise to a leadership position. With narcissists, all that glitters are not gold. You need to know how to protect yourself from all their mind games and manipulation. We have the following tips to protect yourself from the narcissist

How to Spot a Narcissist

This is perhaps the most important part of knowing how to survive narcissism in the workplace. You need to keep yourself updated of the signs of a narcissist so you will not be caught in a bad situation. Narcissists are skilled at blending in to get what they want, and developing your ability to see past their veil will help. They might come off as friendly and charismatic at first. But as we learned, they love making friends with people they can easily take advantage of.

They believe everything they do is under the radar so calling a narcissist out on their behavior might end up backfiring. They like to employ tactics like guilt, gaslighting, and criticism to create any type of chaos they can. Even in professional settings such as the workplace. Watch out for this.

Get Your Facts Right

If he or she is your boss, confrontation may not be the best tactic. They are not against using various dark tactics to confuse and disorient you, creating an unpleasant work situation and eventually getting rid of any threats.

Letting things go is not in their nature. With this in mind, you need to be smarter in your dealings. Keep tabs on everything, all you observed, what they did and said. This will go a long way in protecting you and making a case for your arguments when the time comes.

Guard Your Weaknesses

Empaths and narcissists make a toxic relationship because narcissists see the caring and nurturing nature of the empaths as a weakness. They see these as a loophole to get attached and entangled with them. If the empath knows their forgiving nature could get them into trouble, it's a good plan to keep this fact hidden.

In other words, a narcissist will draw near to you if they feel there is something they can take advantage of. This calls for knowing yourself and your attributes that make you vulnerable. If you trust people easily, have trouble saying no and do things for people freely, the narcissist might explore these traits and use them to their advantage.

Avoid Taking Things Personally

In the world of narcissists, they are the most important person. They do not care about who gets hurt and who they victimize with their games. This is just how they are wired, and it is not your fault. It boils down to the need to put others down to feel better. With this in mind, do not feel sad or bitter if they make derogatory comments, or try to belittle you. It's just their insecurity showing.

Throughout the book, we made sure not to recommend confrontation as with this type of personality it can only end with more problems. You might not win if you call them out. Stroking their ego, while being a step ahead of them is a good way to protect yourself. Keep these points in mind and know how to play your cards right.

Chapter 6 - Healing from Experience with a Narcissist   How to Defeat a Narcissist

Remember that a narcissist is calculated in their actions and behaviors. As a result, you need to be strategic if you want to get your life back. This chapter will explore a proven strategy that will help you break free from the shackles the narcissist has on you. But before proceeding to that, it is important to understand the mind of a narcissist.

How to Understand the Playing Field That Narcissists Thrive On

It is hard, if not impossible, for people in relationships with narcissists to understand, let alone accept that the narcissist's behavior has nothing to do with the victim. They are responsible for their behavior, and we know— wrapping your head around this seems impossible. This is because if someone does anything bad to you, it is logical to conclude that they have a problem with you. In the world of the narcissist, however, this is not true, as humans do not matter. Narcissists usually are at war with themselves and you are just unlucky to be caught in the crossfire.

To a narcissist, you might be no one. The battle is internal, and their goal is to preserve themselves. Hence, even if it seems the narcissist is playing games with you and messing with your head, it is not so. To a narcissist, you are just a tool with which he can hurt himself or make himself feel good. This is hard to understand for many rational beings, because it involves a level of self-preservation so intense that other people become simply pawns. Even though, from an intellectual point of view, we claim to understand it and can explain it to others, emotionally, it will always be a mystery.

We consider the hurt from a narcissist as personal because we examine the motive from our personal perspective. As a result, no matter what, the motive and hurt will be personal to you, and not the narcissist. Why will anyone want to hurt another person? Because deep down inside of them, there is hurt.

The narcissist is aware that you have not done anything to hurt or upset him. However, they see you as a representation of their failure. They have hurt and hatred rooted in their personality, and they know it. Even though narcissists might seem like sadists, they are not in reality. This is because sadists derive enjoyment from the pain and torture they inflict on their victim. Thus, for the torture to work on them, their victim must be thinking and feeling. Narcissists, however, are not wired this way. The pleasure comes from them, rather than from others. Hurting others makes them feel good, since it takes the pressure off of them.

This relationship can be likened to a person punching a bag. The "feel-good" feeling comes when you get a chance to blow off steam, not because you hurt the bag. The bag cannot feel the punches.

This points to the fact that a narcissist does not perceive humans the way other normal and sane people do. Normal people see others as individuals with needs, desires, wishes, motivations, feelings, wants, likes, dislikes, goals, etc. To a narcissist, however, all of this does not make sense—and neither does he care. This is to tell you the extent of how emotionless a narcissist can be. You only matter to a narcissist as long as they can use you—that is all, nothing else matters. Not only does it not matter, he neither recognizes nor acknowledges it. This is why trying to make a narcissist see things from your point of view is a futile effort.

Considering all that has been explained above, it is not surprising that, to a narcissist, his behaviors are not abuse. This is due to the nature of the dysfunction of a narcissist. Truly, a narcissist is under constant attack, even though it is internal. This is why a narcissist can't consider himself as being an abuser, but a victim. Abuse, to a narcissist, could be termed "cooling off" or "blowing off steam." This makes sense since abuse acknowledges the deliberate hurting of others, while blowing off steam does not in any way. It only has to do with the narcissist and his feelings and problems. This makes sense, because that is how they see things. No matter how many punches you throw at a punching bag, you cannot abuse it. Hence, the narcissist truly is not out to get or destroy you, since you are not human (to them). Rather, they care only about protecting themselves. This is shocking and even unbelievable to a rational human being, but this is how the narcissist is wired.

Note that this is only to give you a glimpse of the angle the narcissist is coming from. This is not to excuse or justify their behavior as not abusive; by all means, it is. The narcissist's motives do not matter, because the end result is the same. They are completely self-absorbed, abusive, and manipulative.

Still, this is a good foundation to understand them and their behavior. It can give you a solid grasp of how to handle them better. The idea behind this is not to see the narcissist as the problem, but that deep down inside of the narcissist, something is fundamentally wrong which controls his behavior. This can help you get closure and also realize that it is not about the narcissist, hence, they need to let go and move to a better, healthier, and happier life.

How to Confront a Narcissist in Their Behavior

What is the worst that can happen if you confront a narcissist? Will all hell let loose if you confront him? To really answer this, we need to examine the personality of the parties involved, as well as the circumstances. However, if you do want to confront a narcissist, you need to be clear on what you hope to achieve.

What do you want from this confrontation?

If you have your facts right and you are confident that your partner is a narcissist, you might be tempted to confront them. The sad part, however, is that it is a futile effort. This is because you will be disappointed if you think confronting the narcissist with the information of how they have made your life a living hell will make him change. You might think they would be remorseful or sorry, but it does not work that way.

This is because the emotional capacity of the narcissist is highly underdeveloped. As a result, they cannot understand or process this information, let alone accept the fact that they are not perfect. As a result, a narcissist is not equipped with the ability to search inside his soul and find out the truth.

With the above in mind, before you map out tactics to confront the narcissist, be sure you know what you want from the interaction. If your expectation is fair treatment, equality, and some sense of acceptance in your relationship, it is better you move on. This is because there is little chance of success, and even if you have some, it will be minute, which comes with excessive investment in terms of time and effort.

If you are, however, in a position where moving on is difficult, then you need to arm yourself with useful tactics to make your confrontation fruitful.

Narcissist Reaction to Confrontation

When you confront a narcissist, their default reaction is rage or denial. The narcissist might deny everything, throw tantrums, say you are blowing things out of proportion, and eventually play the victim. Also, expect to have the narcissist turn everything around on you. For instance, if you confront them about spending too much time with the opposite sex, they may say you are too suspicious and do not trust them. If you decide to cope with this treatment, the following steps will help you confront them. However, hoping for any positive turnaround is an illusion. It will only end up setting you up for more pain and disappointment.

When confronting a narcissist, be prepared for the narcissist rage. The rage is their response to the injury that your criticism and disagreement inflicts on their self-esteem. They become enraged because they accept themselves as perfect, without flaws. To a narcissist, a slight disagreement or objection is humiliation. This is why they overreact, become defensive and aggressive, and attack the source of the injury. The person, in turn, suffers with criticism and serious downgrading. They believe in getting even, and if they cannot get even, they will lash out strongly at you in a bid to lessen the impact of the damage to their esteem.

How to Confront?

Sam Vaknin, a self-proclaimed narcissist, advises that the best way is to leave or threaten to leave a narcissist. The threat does not have to be conditional. If they yell at you, yell back at them, slam the door, and be insistent. This will give him a taste of his own medicine.

One of a narcissist's worst nightmares is abandonment. It stands above everything else the narcissist fears. This is why he begins to dread getting emotionally attached to another person. As a result, he misbehaves, acts cruel, and distances himself emotionally from the relationship. Eventually, the abandonment that he so terribly fears comes upon him.

This is the key to confronting a narcissist. Should he give an angry outburst, rage back at him, as well. This rekindles his worst nightmare—abandonment—which makes him come to his senses and he will retreat.

Bear in mind that for you to be successful in confronting a narcissist, you need to be strong. Alongside that, you need to have a good self-esteem and firmly believe you are an individual with rights—you do not deserve such cruel treatments.

How to Protect Yourself from a Narcissist

With an estimation that narcissists make up around 1% of the general population, there is a chance you will come across someone with Narcissistic Personality Disorder in your lifetime. Starting such a relation, however, comes with grave consequences Just like a fish is lured into a bait and pays later with her life, a narcissist lures seemingly innocent people with their charming and romantic behavior. Even though you might not pay with your life, you have a lot to lose. This is why a good defense strategy is to learn how to protect yourself from such individuals. This revolves around training yourself to spot the red flags these individuals emit. In other words, it takes being able to see past their charming personality and captivating talk. In the same way, it is important to protect yourself from falling prey to another narcissist if you recently ended a relationship with one. This involves developing and restoring your core self. In other words, you need to cultivate the healthy practice of connecting to your life. It is about coming up with authentic and healthy ways of relating with yourself, such that what attracted you to the narcissist is gone.

Know Who a Narcissist is

This is the first step in knowing how to protect yourself from a narcissist. You cannot keep yourself away from what you do not know. This is where many people miss it. They have such faith in the goodness of man in general that it is impossible for them to accept that some people could be so callous, mean, and emotionless.

Many people are also fond of giving strangers the benefit of the doubt. However, equipping yourself with the idea of who a narcissist is and how they behave can go a long way in saving yourself months, years, or even a lifetime of misery.

If you have come this far with this manual, I believe you already have an idea of the kind of person a narcissist is. As a summary, keep an eye out for red flags like your partner constantly feeling like they are better than everyone else, with a conviction that they cannot be wrong; someone who takes excessive pride in their accomplishments; reveals a desperate need for admiration; or behaves in a cocky, patronizing, demanding, and self-absorbed manner.

Connect to Your Mind and Body

To protect yourself from a narcissist, you need to be happy and comfortable with yourself. This involves knowing what you want, what you want to be, how you want others to perceive you, and having access to your inner resources. This authenticity allows them respond with wisdom to all the tactics of the narcissist, rather than with fear.

Narcissist do not like the truth and people in tune with their inner being is a strong repellant to them. Hence, to defeat a narcissist is not about the ability to argue and reason things out. By the time a narcissist employs cruel tactics like gaslighting, your ability to reason will be crushed. In fact, some narcissists love the challenge of conquering strong and passionate women.

Strive to Know Yourself

An authentic person has a lifelong mission of knowing and understanding themselves. This helps them understand others, which guides their life, relations, and interactions. This makes them happy and contented with life and all it has to offer, while striving to improve themselves. Connecting with yourself allows you to develop a unique understanding of yourself and others. When you consider a narcissist, they cannot engage in normal conversation. If you have ever had deep conversations (hopes, dreams, fears, etc.) with a narcissist, with the hope that they will reason, love, and empathize with you, you are wrong. All he is interested in is information with which he can control and use against you with time.

With an authentic person, however, a narcissist is powerless. This is due to their inability to spot loopholes to prey on, to instill fear, gaslight, and manipulate. The narcissist detests being seen for who they really are. They do not like being seen as emotionally weak, because in their mind, showing love and being compassionate is for the weak.

Have a Strong Inner Sense of Control

True happiness comes from within, and authentic people know this. As a result, they can enjoy the peace and tranquility they seek. This gives them the capacity to detach their emotions from issues that they know are the narcissist's. They can deal with and control personal issues, and also separate these from the narcissists, irrespective of how the narcissist tries to manipulate them.

They are aware of the tactics the narcissist employs, so despite everything the narcissist does, they can relax and prevent upsetting emotions from springing up. This is not surprising, since it is normal for the narcissist to always try to make their partner panic. It is common for the narcissist to be stuck in a cycle of making their partner take the fall of all wrongdoings. For instance:

• Behaving like they are not receiving adequate love and attention

• Feel like it is their right to treat others badly

• Make others responsible for their own woes

• Expect to be treated as if they are special

A narcissist is not interested in healing and getting better. To them, this is for the weak, as they do not even believe anything is wrong with them. Hence, a real person will not be surprised by these behaviors and will not even expect improvement. As a result, they know that the best way to handle them is to keep their own emotions in check. In other words, they are not surprised each time the narcissist acts irrationally. Many people are shocked and disturbed when the narcissist misbehaves, because they expect better. Yet, over time, their actions and behaviors have followed the same pattern—expecting an improvement is setting oneself up for disappointment. When the narcissist, however, sees that all his action has no effect on you, your fear system refuses to be activated, they are starved of what keeps them fulfilled. With time, they will let you be.

Make What Hurts and Makes You Vulnerable a Secret

Vulnerable emotions are part of what makes us human. It is vital to a balanced life and should only be shared with people you trust—not a narcissist. This is because emotions that make us vulnerable are important sources of power that make us human.

A narcissist's mindset and view of others around is way different from that of normal people. He might put up an act to show as if he cares about your problem, but he's gathering information about you. These are data that he will use to manipulate you, instill fear, confuse your thinking faculties, etc. In other words, to you, you feel you are pouring your heart to someone while the narcissist is nothing more than a scientist gathering data.

Stay Firm and Grounded

We all have an intuition that knows things even without much fact. People might call this gut or sixth senses. Your gut can warn you of dangers and give you strong feelings when you are trying to make a decision. Hence, if you meet someone and they appear too good to be true, listen to your gut.

Narcissist are charming, sometimes with charisma and an outgoing personality. This is often in a bid to bait unsuspecting people. If your sixth sense is warning you, draw the curtain.

When next you are with someone who makes you question your self-worth, remind yourself of how important and special you are. Make it a personal rule to take your time in getting to know someone. Do not be caught in the drama and do not feel compelled to explain your values life choices to the narcissist. Remember, they only care about getting you entangled in their web, to use you as a source for their evil whims.

How to Break Up With a Narcissist

Dating a narcissist is draining and exhausting. This is not surprising, because of their vain, manipulative, self-absorbed, competitive, and proud nature. To break up with a narcissist, you need to be well prepared. Bear in mind that rejection does not go well with a narcissist. as they are likely to view it as an attack and respond with strong backlash and hostility—no matter how careful you are.

In dealing with a narcissist, you need to be smart. A narcissist might not even attack you. On the contrary, he might break down, sob, and plead with the promise to change, appealing to your compassionate side not to sever the tie.

You might not be able to predict the narcissist reaction. However, it is important to take important steps to protect yourself and tactically end such a toxic relationship.

Before the Breakup

Breaking up with a narcissist is dealing a big blow to their pride. Hence, humiliation is not negotiable, if and when you reject a narcissist. As a result, prepare your mind for drama as they will likely try to turn the tables around, dominating the conversation.

The key here is limiting the time you spend on the breakup, and make sure it is done in the company of friends or loved ones. This makes the situation less dramatic.

During the Conversation

In breaking up with a narcissist, you need to outsmart them. This is not a time for honesty, because they will manipulate what you say and even use it against you. This is not the time to rant about how they have made your life a living hell, or how they have ruined everything. Neither should you tell them how much they are suffocating you. Rather, tell them you are not good for each other, and the relationship is not working for either of you.

Assigning blame will not do any good here, as narcissists are good at playing defense when they feel at fault. The idea is to make the reason for the breakup as vague and general as possible. Keep the list of hurts and cons to yourself.

Having established this foundation, how do you go about severing the tie with your narcissist partner?

Chapter 7 - How to Get Over Them in Real Life

Dealing with the Aftermath

After encounters with a psychopath, one of the most common problems empaths face is their (often accurate) perception of the injustice of how they were treated. We can examine ways to get over the ruin by looking at specific situations, like the following:

'I am recently separated and upset by the unfairness of the entire situation. My ex got the money, a new woman and a happy life, and I am left with nothing. I am emotionally shattered and destroyed. How do I overcome this exceedingly unfair outcome?'

It may seem unbearably unfair on the surface, but look deeper. Don't undersell the most valuable commodities that money just can't buy:

Freedom

Time

Inner truth

Don't be jealous of the new partner. She's actually the victim. You are free to do anything now. You can rebuild, with a valuable lesson behind you. It can only get better from this point. At best (if the psychopath loves the new partner in the only way they know how) she will be owned and controlled like a possession and pet, with no freedom to direct her life. Over the long term, it's a psychological prison with dangerous consequences. At worst, the new target will be robbed of her money, trust, sanity, energy and possibly health. She may be completely broken, a shadow of her former self. When she gets out, she's in for at least 12 months of deep recovery. You, now, have everything open to you.

Don't be jealous of him or his life. Psychopaths never learn and they never grow. They are trapped in a losing cycle dependent on the uncertain winds of fate.

Weak foundations – The psychopath has never developed the patience, work ethic and character foundations that result in satisfying rewards. The sad thing is that they never will. Their motto will always be 'immediate gratification of the self', by deception and conning others.

Destroying their own futures – Just as they're incapable of considering anyone else's long-term interest, they're actually incapable of considering their own. Making enemies and spreading bitterness shoots them in the foot over the long-term. They underestimate certain individuals' future capacity for influence, power and success, or their will-power to get even.

Delusional thinking – Although most psychopaths feel no love and loyalty to anyone, they expect unconditional love and loyalty from those over whom they've established a dominance bond. Anything less is a justification for them to act out. This belief system is delusional. In real life, can such expectations ever result in interpersonal happiness? It's a hopeless, perpetual lose-lose cycle.

Outer image, built upon sand – The only way the psychopath can continue their convincing presentation of success is by pulling increasingly bigger scams on unsuspecting targets. Always, underneath the presentation, they are pure, hollow frauds. They can't control or change themselves internally for lasting fulfillment or success, and consequently, their illusory success depends on external factors that are outside of their own control. It's only a matter of time when things catch up with them – typically by offending the wrong powers, being involved in an incident that exposes their backgrounds or mistaking an eagle for a lamb.

Can never feel the nourishment of love, truth, spiritual wisdom – Psychopaths are stuck with being a black hole, eternally empty. They need to constantly fill this hole up with external things, temporary thrills. They will always live somewhat aimlessly, never experiencing a fulfilling life with purpose in their heart, or the soul-enriching quality of love and affection. And in most cases, they contribute very little to the world.

Is this really an enviable way to live?

But you are a rechargeable battery, capable of change. You are capable of building foundations that are the pillars of lasting happiness. And thus you possess infinite future possibilities in finding love, success and fulfillment.

You may have been robbed temporarily, simply because you didn't know these types of people existed. No matter how shattered you may be, you will recover – you just don't know it yet. You can overcome the temporary setback by taking positive action and moving forward.

It doesn't matter how pretty the presentation is. The core of the psychopath's ethos is a fraud. Once you get over the emotional aspect of the situation, and see their core for what they truly are, they are losers and poor investments for you.

Don't be jealous of their life together. Psychopathic individuals are masters of impression management. They live a double life – a false, confident personality on the outside, and an internal ugliness that's bound to comes out sooner or later, through the illusions. Photographs and constant Facebook updates are just that, illusions. How do we know that's really their reality? It generally takes two healthy people to have a happy relationship. One toxic person and a new, naïve source of supply are not the ingredients that bode well for long-term happiness.

The glamorous illusion and the sad reality can be seen in the example of Manohara Odella Pinot, a 17-year-old Indonesian model who married a Malaysian prince and became a royal princess. In magazines, TV and from afar, she seemed extremely lucky, achieving the pinnacle of what every girl in Indonesia aspired to. But after Ms. Pinot escaped, she alleged that she was treated like an animal and a sex slave, her husband's property. She claimed that she had been isolated in a foreign country with no friends or relatives, and injected with tranquilizers by guards and doctors to be kept in the bedroom. Under threats of beatings, she was forced to maintain a happy facade at public events. "After the first minute of the marriage solemnization, he quickly changed into a psychopath. It was true that he wanted to separate me from my mother," Manohara said.

Be glad for freedom. You have time, the most precious resource, free from bondage and unperturbed by toxic individuals. Don't let it go to waste.

Now the question is, what will you do with your freedom, precious time, and new-found inner truth?

How to Avoid Facebook, Social Media and All Reminders

During the healing stage, to protect your own wellbeing, make an absolute rule not to look at that person's or their friends' Facebook pages. This is for two reasons:

1. For a psychopath, appearance is everything. That's all they have. It's almost an instinctual behavior to put on a front of success and happiness, no matter what the truth is. No matter what happens, their Facebook and social media profiles will always be plastered with illusions – looking happy, successful, even if they are heading to prison tomorrow. Once you understand the fakeness, it's comical, and pitiful. The sneak peek will only serve to make you feel bad about your situation, or to trigger bad memories.

2. Once a psychopath is done with you and has moved on to a new target, they engineer the job interview process we looked at all over again, with a brand new persona designed to work a new target. Consequently, their Facebook identity may all of sudden become an opposite identity. Their interests, religion and personality may change completely, and pictures of their new performance will be everywhere. You don't

need to be involved or be reminded of any of these crazy antics.

It's best to destroy all physical traces of their existence. Block all calls, texts, emails; get rid of all physical reminders of them, avoid accidental meetings and places that remind you of them. Implement tactics so that they don't have the means to keep tabs on your life.

How to Establish NCEA (No Contact Ever Again) Strategically

Establishing NCEA in tiered steps or stages works the best. Psychologically, sometimes you need to trick yourself to make sure you adhere to what's best for you.

1. Make a promise to yourself not to establish contact until you are completely over that person, and they have no further power to affect any of your emotions. Think of this as something temporary you must do, not permanent. It may take a couple of months or even years, but give yourself the gift to heal unperturbed in the best environment possible. Then take action to focus 100% on your healing and your happiness. Do not attempt any contact until you arrive at a point where your emotions towards the psychopath become complete indifference.

2. Sooner or later, you will be over it. When you are sufficiently distanced from the excruciating dramas, then it's the time to be rational about things. If the urge comes up, review the lists recommended later on – and make a rational cost/benefit analysis to see whether the risks are worth it.

3. You will likely find the longer you stay away from the toxicity, the more you can allow the sunshine back into your life again – your heart will feel warm, glowing and radiant once again. When you eventually notice this, be sure to record this transition or moment in time. This will help you remember to stay centered and never to allow external influences to destroy your hard-won serenity and happiness.

How to Adopt the Standard of a Blissful Constant

This original idea was adapted from the book Psychopath Free by Peace. It aims at having a solid baseline through ties with a person who inspires feelings of heartwarming love, trust and reliability. That private baseline can be used as a measurement to weed out negative people from your life.

Steps to Obtaining a Constant

1. Think of someone you love and who loves you. It can be family, friends, a deceased someone or even a pet. The important thing is that the person or entity you pick as a Constant should always make you feel safe and peaceful. They should possess qualities you admire, such as kindness and compassion.

2. Now ponder three questions for yourself.

How do you feel around your Constant?

Does your Constant make you feel anxious, jealous, insecure and other bad emotions?

What is the difference between your Constant and people who make you feel awful or unbalanced?

3. When you meet people with negative energy, recall the positivity your Constant brings out in you.

Remember that you are not crazy. After all, you are totally normal around your Constant. Not only that, you are the best version of yourself.

Understand that good people make you feel good, and bad people make you feel bad.

4. Decide whether you still want to be around people who bring out negativity in you.

How to Embrace the Power of Lists

This exercise involves structuring your thoughts about what is often an emotionally loaded, painful topic through writing a series of tailored lists. It is powerful and incredibly therapeutic.

First, it utilizes how our brain naturally converts information. When you write things down, your brain automatically converts the emotionally incomprehensible to become logically comprehensible. However, when you verbalize the past in continuing 'talking about it', you may relive the trauma and emotional turmoil all over again. Detaching and comprehending is one of the first paths to healing.

Second, these lists take your mind off of a toxic past, and onto a new world of unlimited, positive potentials. You will be able to embrace new ideas and endeavors that are now open to you. The best part is you can gain this instant freedom and feeling of hope simply by reviewing your lists again and again.

The first batch of lists focus on rationality – so as to separate reality from illusion and see the truth with clarity.

1. Make a list of everyone you know personally that you really admire – people of generosity, genuineness,

strong moral compasses, substance and courage.; people who are doing amazing, admirable, great things in life. They might be family members, friends, old bosses, or co-workers. Now compare your real-life heroes to the psychopath in terms of character, actions, life goals, and how they make others feel. Would your real-life heroes do what the psychopath did?

This comparison tactic really does work and is quite powerful. The psychopath compared you against everyone else: isn't it time to compare them against your heroes?

When you take your mind away from their illusory persona, and the emotions of the situation, the psychopath comes up as, well, just pretty much scum – disgusting and kind of worthless in comparison to people who deserve respect.

This is how you direct your thoughts from here on in, not through the manufactured persona that created artificial desirability.

2. Write down all the reasons that you miss the psychopath.

3. Write all the reasons that it is better that he or she is out of your life.

The next batch puts the focus back on you – on your happiness and self-improvement. It gives you something bigger to focus on. Your life is worth so much more. It is much bigger than one toxic and temporary situation.

1. Write what you want to achieve, in terms of short-term, medium-term, and long term goals.

2. Write down everything you are passionate about.

3. Write down everything that you are grateful for (family, friends, personal skillsets, past achievements, present enjoyments and so on). During our down time, we don't see the gifts we already have that make our lives wonderful; the qualities that no one can ever permanently take away.

4. What do you love about yourself? Celebrate your good qualities.

Now the last two lists are inner reflections that ensures the lessons learned stay with you for the rest of your life. You may need some time and introspection before you are ready. But once you have the lists down, you will always have a precious reminder to safeguard your personal well-being, values and long-term happiness.

1. Write a list of what attracted you to the psychopath in the first place. Was it looks? Promises of true love?

Attention? A need to be needed? A need to feel approval? A desire to reform someone? A fear of being alone? Use this list to understand what is inside of you that made you vulnerable to them in the first place. Get to know yourself so you won't be blind-sided again by a future invader that provides little value.

2. Lastly, make a list of priority qualities before you look for someone new to date. Focus on internal qualities that are important to you. But keep this list to yourself and don't advertise what you are looking for, as a predator can quickly assume that persona.

Now review these lists weekly, or whenever you think of the psychopath. Eventually, your brain will automatically adjust 180 degrees. You will be happy they are out of your life, while focusing towards the thing that truly matters – you.

Chapter 8 - Building Healthy Relationships

As much as you might have heard or read about narcissists, you are not wrong to build a relationship with one. You also need to know that you are not deliberately setting yourself on the path of self-destruction. Narcissists are quite romantic and can be really charming. They are great lovers and can be friends. The truth is they can be sensitive to how you feel and adjust to your needs.

However, narcissists can be very manipulative, and they are complicated people; therefore, being in any sort of relationship, whether romantic or not, platonic or professional, you need to know that it can be confusing and be set for the situation. Narcissists are complicated and hard to understand because sometimes you will find them very helpful and dependable to point they will seem to care about you. The truth is their devotion and kindness is mostly to benefit themselves and further put them in control of things.

Forming a relationship with a narcissist is not uncommon. Many people are in such a narcissistic relationship without even realizing it until they are far into it. A victim doesn't feel like leaving because his or her life is centered on the narcissist. It is difficult to let go of such a relationship. It could be because they are married and have kids. Also at times, dealing with an ex who is a narcissist can be quite difficult.

Narcissists are potentially harmful in many ways. How do you simply make the relationship work? How is it possible to build a healthy relationship with a narcissist? It is indeed possible and maybe rewarding to have a relationship with someone who is a narcissist, but that relationship would be psychologically and emotionally draining. A narcissist usually lacks what it takes to build a strong relationship. They do not show consistent kindness, compassion, selflessness, reciprocity, compromise, and empathy. They drain the energy and spirit from their supposed partners, turning them to figurative punching bags.

What to Expect in a Relationship with a Narcissist

Being in a relationship or having any link with a narcissist has many challenges like I have earlier said, but when you are aware of some of the things to expect, you should know how to handle the relationship better to build a healthy one.

You Will Need to Make Some Sacrifices

To be able to have a fairly good life or relationship with a narcissist, you need lots of sacrifices to keep the relationship going. You will sacrifice a part of you, especially your beliefs and what you stand for, and one of the expected constants is that you will be lied to over and over yet must accept it.

Narcissists are crafty and very manipulative. They are good at changing narratives and altering reality into the version that suits them, and in the end, they get you to agree to something that you didn't do. To keep narcissists happy, you will need to learn how to accept their version of reality as the truth of what has happened even when it is not. That way, you will always escape their fury and not be on the receiving end.

Part of the sacrifice is that you might never get praised for achieving something or rewarded for behaving well. Narcissists will at every opportunity try to undermine your effort. They are so manipulative to the point where they call all the shots yet in a very shrewd way that will seem as though you are in control. They will let you make decisions but will do something totally different, and you have to appreciate them for doing that.

Building healthy relationships with narcissists mean you have to play a secondary role. You need to make sacrifices that will drain you in a lot of ways.

To a Narcissist, No One Is to Be Trusted

Narcissists wouldn't trust anybody except themselves. Even when you do everything right and have never given them any reason not to trust you, they would still not respect you enough to allow you to lead your life without interference and surveillance, and they can go to the extent of spying and stalking you.

Narcissists have the habit of tracking their partners. In a romantic relationship, narcissists are likely to install trackers without the knowledge of their partners. It could be on their phone or computer, and they feel no remorse about it but rather proud of their action.

Regrettably, most narcissists abuse drugs and/or alcohol to the extreme. Their partners will have to endure and adapt to their lifestyle and live with the perpetual fear and expectation that they may take things too far with the drugs or alcohol and act unpredictably.

Most narcissists usually develop bad habits and, because of that, can become so irresponsible, missing their appointments, meetings, and work. Therefore, it puts their partners in situations where they have to clean up the mess they create and make up excuses to absolve them. The reason is that the partners have been conditioned to believe that they are a team and that it's them against the whole world.

Narcissists will never put their trust in anyone; therefore, they use words that will keep their victims spellbound like "You are my world" and "Without you, I'm nothing." That way, their victims are comforted with a false sense of security. Meanwhile, they are just cutting their partners from everyone and everything, pitching them against the world and using them. Narcissists will say things and take actions that will be convincing enough to make you believe in them. Trust them and risk it all for them. You should be ready not to be trusted when in a relationship with a narcissist. Although it is not really clear if narcissists do things with the intention of hurting their partners to the level they do, they give the excuse of having a bad childhood, and it is your duty to understand and forgive them for all their shortcomings and behaviors. They will explode, and you will face their rage if you don't forgive them of everything they have done, including the times they abused you.

You Will Be Drained and Tapped Out

Narcissists don't like taking the blame for anything. They look for someone else to take the blame, and you who have a relationship with one will likely be the one to fill that role. Therefore, to make your relationship work, you will have to come to terms with the fact that you are a scapegoat at every opportunity and probably be demeaned. And if you don't want to take the blame for them, the narcissistic traits will kick in, and they will accuse you of being crazy and inconsiderate. Mostly, all your feelings will be used against you to make you feel bad.

To make such a relationship work, you should be ready to put your self-interest behind you and be prepared to be harassed because everything that is wrong is your fault. You will need to lose yourself. The things you love, the things you like, the fun things you do, your music choice, books, and movies will all be termed bad or uncool. For them, you have a terrible taste. They will gradually mold you into somebody you are not.

To keep narcissists happy, you might have to lose your friends, family, and even your job. You might have to stop pursuing your career. Basically, you will have to live for them to be happy. Your life will revolve around them to keep the relationship going and narcissists happy. You stay home all day doing chores. However, all that won't get you some accolades. They will then term you a boring person.

Some narcissists will rather have you keep your job so that you can help keep their lifestyle financed, milking you while you slave for their happiness.

Your time is one of the greatest gifts you can ever give to someone. This is a world where time is money and of the essence. We usually don't have the time to spend with our loved ones. But giving time and energy to someone you care about can hold the relationship together. That way, you will have time to fix all the problems that may arise even if you get blamed.

Tips and Tools to Maintain a Healthy Relationship

You are on the path of managing narcissists. The following tips should be incorporated into your daily dealings with narcissists. With time, narcissists should start getting used to the changes, and possibly, you will notice a change in them too.

"We" Should Be Used as Often as Possible

Whenever it is possible, try using the word "we," and then strongly emphasize relationships during communications. According to research from Rethinking Narcissism: The Bad—and Surprising Good—about Feeling Special, this simple method actually works well on narcissists. The research indicates that narcissists were given passages that are filled with words like "our," "we," and "us." When they were done with the passage, the narcissists were actually moved and were willing to help other people in need and also became less obsessed with their ideas of being the center of attention.

Reward Good Behavior

Make it a point to observe and compliment the narcissist when you notice they are warm. Give them compliments for their warmth. However, do not compliment them for their performance or their achievement. It only makes them want to manipulate and dominate you more.

When you notice they are warm, give them compliments. You can compliment them for being warm, not for their performance or achievement. Be observant and look for moments that the narcissist demonstrates a better behavior and emphasize on it. Pushing a narcissist to the center means emphasizing on the moments that they show some kind of ability to collaborate, show interest in people, or concern and care for the people around them. In fact, whenever they behave more communal, reward them.

Differentiate Good and Bad Behaviors

When you compliment, does it help? If it does, then you can take it up a notch. You should tactically contrast their good behavior with their bad behavior. Contrasting both behaviors is more or less like catching, except you are recounting the past and present the same time. If you do have any of such behavior, note it. It is far more effective when it is contrasted with some recollection of communal behavior.

For example: "Our time with the club members last week was really exciting, and it was a wonderful experience when everyone got the time to express and contribute to the course, although today everyone had lesser chances, which were not so terrific for us. Can we give it a shot like we did last week?"

This method will subtly point out the past and present at the same time, suggesting a change without tampering with the narcissist's ego. When you point a bad behavior, make sure to pair it with one of the narcissist's good behaviors. That way, you can make your submission.

Let Them Know How You Feel

First and foremost, tell the narcissist how you feel. As you feel unhappy, uneasy, and uncomfortable, use the word "I." For instance, "I am unhappy about your actions." You can use more impactful words like "scared," "afraid," and "sad," but if you are not in a romantic relationship with the narcissist, a less intense language might be better to use. Always go with your gut. The goal here is to describe your experience to narcissists and let them know their behavior that is causing it.

You can let narcissists know how they affect you and how they make you feel. Mention their bad behavior and the likely corrections you want to see.

There are different characteristics and types of narcissists. There are those who are covert, communal, grandiose, extreme, and many more. However, there is one thing that they share, which is the need to feel special.

As humans, we are bound to make mistakes. You don't have to put up a false front to express denial. Making mistakes is totally natural, so trying to show that you are perfect will only earn you envy. Instead, you should show your true self.

Instead, show others your true self. Sometimes, you may look stupid, but it's normal. People who truly care about you will be empathic toward you and eventually grow closer to you. Striving to look special in the eyes of people will make people who actually care about you avoid you. So you should open up to them and have all kinds of specialness you deserve.

Once you have done the above (pointing out their shortcomings), let them know the corrections you are expecting. You should know the kind of changes you want, and it should be done in the form of coaching. It's just like teaching narcissists what they need to do to improve interactions. You can use statements like "Can you tell me what you want?" "Can you bring down your voice?" or "Can you not do this in front of people?" You can let them know how unhappy you feel when you are being embarrassed in front of other people.

Understand and Accept Differences

To build a healthy relationship, it is very important that we frankly accept our differences. We need to understand that everyone is unique and different in many ways. If we understand that we all perceive the world in different ways, then we might as well have crossed one of the greatest challenges in building relationships.

People often feel better when they feel other people understand them and are in tune with their point of view. On the other hand, however, life would generally be boring and dull if we all think and act the same. Understanding and accepting that we are all wired differently, making us unique, will be a very strong foundation on which we can build healthy relationships.

Listen and Pay Attention

The art of listening is a skill that improves relationships, perception, and understanding. When you listen and give attention, the other person will feel proud and confident. They will feel supported. They will feel heard. Responsive interactions can promote healthy relationships. That way, the parties can communicate and understand each other better. You shouldn't aim to just be a listener though. Be an active listener during conversations. Use body language by making eye contact, nodding to show that you agree with the speaker, and even asking questions for clarification if needed.

Also, you should listen to what others say without interrupting them. Take your time to ruminate. Think of your response and give your answer. Answering questions without thinking will do you no good. You will notice a positive difference once you get used to listening to others while they speak.

While listening, try to paraphrase your understanding of what the message means and then reflect the message to the person for further verification. That way, it shows you have been paying attention. This process of verification and getting feedback is what shows that you are an active listener. It draws other people close to you and makes them trust you.

Develop Empathy

This is the ability to relate and understand other people's feelings. This is important because when you put yourself in other people's shoes, you get to understand them. You get to find a solution to problems that someone is facing since you already understand the situation.

If you want to be treated nicely, then you should treat others nicely and vice versa. Therefore, it is important to treat others the way we want to be treated. Being there for others always bring a positive return.

Empathy is like a bridge that helps people build healthy relationships. Empathy deals with perceiving and connecting to the feelings and needs of another person on a deeper level where you can understand their inner state without judging or blaming. But interpret those feelings in a way that suggests support, understanding, and mutual trust.

Be Compassionate

People who are compassionate are always conscious of the sufferings other people go through and have this in-built desire to help them lessen their burden.

Compassion is a social skill that will really help you because there is this notion that people who are compassionate care about other people a lot, and everybody always wants to be with people who care. You know what narcissism is and you know how to deal with it. The next step is making sure that you have what is needed to truly heal from the experience. This is a process, and no one expects you to just forget the issue never happened. Working on yourself and putting yourself first is what will allow you to get over the negative consequences of your experience.

Personal Self-Esteem

When someone has low self-esteem, they are more vulnerable to narcissists and other people and situations that are largely negative. In fact, narcissists look for those with low self-esteem because they know that it will make it easier to get them into their web. When you have good self-esteem, you have a healthy level of self-respect and confidence in your abilities and worth. When self-esteem is low, someone is more likely to tolerate abusive situations, not live up to their potential and become depressed.

When you have high self-esteem, you:

Feel accepted and valued by others

Respect and accept yourself even when you are making mistakes

Recognize your positive qualities

Think positively concerning yourself

Feel worthy of be given respect and fairness by others

Believe in yourself and do not allow setbacks or failure stop you from pursuing your goals

Take pride in what you do

Low self-esteem is characterized by:

Putting more focus on your failures instead of your accomplishments

Feeling inferior or insecure

Feeling that others will automatically not accept you

Thinking negatively about yourself

Being very hard on yourself when it is not warranted

Feeling like you do not deserve good things because you think you are defective in some way

Doubting your ability to be successful

Self-esteem is a part of everything that you do in life. It affects your performance at school, work and in your relationships. Low self-esteem can also stop you from living a full life since it is characterized by fear to try new things or test your limits.

Where Self-Esteem Comes From

Self-esteem ultimately comes from within. However, there are a number of factors that can influence it. The people around you play a role in how you see yourself. This is especially true when it comes to those close to you and those you respect. For example, if a parent is constantly critical of a child, this can damage the child's self-esteem. On the other hand, when a parent is very supportive, it helps someone to see their own value which leads to healthy self-esteem.

Every person has that inner voice that essentially tells them what to think of themselves. For some, this inner voice can be highly negative and critical. When this happens, it is easy to believe the voice and feel as though you are inferior. It is common to have negative feelings, but when you allow them to dominate, you eventually start believing them. It is important to listen to negative inner feelings, but then put them into perspective. For example, you did poorly on a test, so naturally, this is upsetting. If your inner voice tells you that you are a failure and you listen to it and do not question it, you will start to believe this, resulting in lower self-esteem.

Comparing yourself to other people is another influencer on your self-esteem. It is fine to evaluate those around you, but do not allow this to overshadow your strengths. Taking inventory of your weaknesses and strengths and focusing on what you are good can help prevent the strengths of those around you from negatively impacting how you view yourself.

Other factors that can alter your self-esteem include:

How people react to you

Illness, injury, and disability

Status and role in society

Your personal life experiences

Age

Media messages

The media is a major influencer. For example, you see all of these seemingly perfect people in magazines and on television. It is natural for people to compare themselves and believe that what they are seeing is what they need to be. This can be especially damaging to younger children and those who already have low self-esteem. It is important to remember that every person is unique and there is no right way to look.

Improving Your Self-Esteem

The good news is that if you have low self-esteem, this does not have to remain. There are ways to boost it and alleviate the negative thoughts and feelings from dominating your view of yourself. To get started, work on developing life skills that contribute to how you see yourself and the world around you. These include:

Do not be afraid to identify and experience your feelings. When you push feelings down and try to ignore them, they will eventually come to the surface.

Do not be afraid to detach yourself from negative situations and people.

Be receptive to those around you and empathize with people.

Think optionally and not in black and white. This allows you to solve problems better and learn new things.

Be assertive when it is needed. Do not allow others to dictate the direction of your life.

Focus on the good things in your life and what you are good at. Low self-esteem can make it seem like you are not good enough at anything. However, when you reflect on the good, it makes it easier to remember that it does exist on days when you are feeling down.

Make a learning opportunity out of every mistake. Every person fails and makes mistakes. This is part of life. However, do not dwell on these and the negative consequences that might come with them. Spend an hour being upset because it is important to experience your emotions. However, after an hour, go into action mode and consider why the mistake or failure occurred. You will always be able to find at least one lesson. This lesson reduces the risk of mistakes and failure in the future.

Know that perfection is simply not possible. What is important is that you are putting in the effort and working to learn and get better. No person is born automatically being great at everything. Life is all about learning and working on developing the skills needed to achieve your goals.

Remember that every person has their own strengths. Imagine a world where every person is just good at everything. There would be no healthy competition, no learning, and no balance. Know your strengths and respect the strengths of others.

Know what you cannot change. For example, if you are short, you are short. You cannot change this. Once you accept what cannot be changed, you can start putting your focus on the areas of your life that can be improved.

Do not be afraid to try. You never know what you are good at until you test your limits. Have you always wanted to play soccer, but were afraid you were not good enough? Get a game going with friends or join a local team. You may be great, or you may not. Either way, you tried it, and every new thing you try expands your horizons.

Give yourself credit when you deserve it. When you do something great, be proud of yourself. It is easy to put more focus on flaws because this is just what humans do. However, when you switch your focus to the good stuff, your self-esteem will get a boost.

How to Heal from Narcissism in Your Life

Dealing with a narcissist in your life can be damaging, and it allows for a flood of negativity in your life. Once the narcissist is gone, the issues you faced do not just disappear with them. You have to take the time to heal, and this can take some time. Give yourself time and be patient with yourself. There are stages that you go through during the healing process. Learning more about these allow you to ensure that you are doing everything needed to truly heal.

During the first stage, denial is common. You do not want to believe that the narcissist in your life is a toxic

144

person. You may make excuses for their behavior and not want to admit that they are not healthy for you. Start writing down your thoughts concerning their treatment of you. Every few days, look back at what you wrote. This allows you to identify the pattern.

The second stage involves getting to know more about narcissism. This allows you to see what they do, and it allows you to realize that they are not capable of empathy and healthy relationships. This is a hard lesson to learn, but it is imperative for you to heal.

The third stage starts the separation process. Write a letter telling the narcissist in your life that you are walking away. Be detailed about why you are walking away. Now, you will not send the letter. This is for you to find some closure as you end the relationship.

For stage four, you cut the person from your life. Once you say "goodbye" you have to remain strong. Cut off all contact and do not give into them no matter what. It is common for a narcissist to try and manipulate you back into their life. You should consider a clean break. This means that you just cut off contact and never go back. Since this requires taking your attention away from them, expect them to try and contact you. They can be very persistent. Just make sure that you never respond.

Stage five involves taking a deep look at why you started a relationship with them in the first place. What was it about the narcissist that made you want them in your life? This can help you to prevent a future experience with a narcissist. It also lets you reflect and determine if your reasons for a relationship with them are things you need to work on. For example, was your self-esteem low when you started spending time with them? If so, improving your self-esteem can prevent a future narcissist experience.

The sixth stage is all about you. You want to evaluate your weaknesses and your self-worth. Find places that need improvement and dedicate yourself to working on them. After having a narcissist in your life, it is common to be in a negative place. Take small steps to essentially recover from your experience. Every person gets through their step in their own time. Do not rush and do not get discouraged if you are going through the motions slowly. Every day is another day without narcissism in your life.

The seventh and final stage is accepting that the situation happened and commit yourself to learning from it. Use the pain and negativity that the narcissist caused in your life to be stronger and to drive you to put the focus on self-care. You do not need anyone in your life that contributes anything negative. Remember this. You are valuable and worthy. You also want to truly forgive yourself.

How to Handle Future Narcissism in Your Life

This ultimately comes down to knowing your worth and putting up your boundaries with any narcissist you might meet in the future. With improved self-esteem and knowing how to approach those who are narcissistic, you can better avoid falling into their web and having your life filled with their negativity.

First and foremost, make a pact with yourself that you will never allow another narcissist to take control over you. You are valuable, and your worth is determined by you and not them. They can quickly worm their way into your life because they are charming. It is easy to not believe a narcissist is actually a narcissist at first. They can be initially nice, or at least seem that way based on their actions and their desire to control and manipulate you.

Consider your past experience with a narcissist. Do you remember how the relationship began? Look for similar patterns with any new person in your life who you think might be a narcissist. Remembering history is one of the best ways to prevent issues from your past from repeating themselves. It can be hard to spot the signs at first, so be diligent and do not discount your feelings if you think another narcissist has entered your life.

Go to your support system and people you trust. Ask their opinion about the person you think might be a narcissist. In many cases, when you are getting close to someone, it can be difficult to see their flaws. However, your close friends and family are on the outside looking it and can pick up on issues faster and easier than you can. Just remember that if their opinions are negative, do not get defensive. They care about you and want to ensure that you are surrounded by good people.

Practice regular self-care. When you are taking care of yourself and putting yourself first, you are less vulnerable to the charms and manipulations of a narcissist. There are numerous ways to practice self-care. You can choose one or several methods depending on your needs and what you want. The following are common self-care methods to consider:

Make your schedule simpler so that you can put more focus on the activities that make you happy and alleviate your stress.

Take a warm bath and use this time to read a book, listen to your favorite songs or just kick back. Make sure the atmosphere is relaxing and that this is time just for you. Turn off your phone and eliminate any distractions.

Get some physical activity since this will help to boost your physical, mental and emotional health. It is a good way to blow off some steam. Any type of physical activity that you enjoy will provide you with benefits.

Create a list of what you are grateful for. A narcissist can take away your joy, so sometimes you need to remind yourself of the things in your life that are great.

Find a mentor that can aid you in getting to know yourself and guide you through difficult times. This can be a religious leader, a therapist or any person in this realm.

Take a day to unplug from everything. Turn off all electronics and go back to a simpler time. Take a walk or a nap, enjoy favorite foods, play games with friends or anything else that does not require electronics.

Try something new. Have you been wanting to start painting or write a book? Is there a type of cuisine you have not tried before? As long as it is something new to you, do it. This gets you out of your comfort zone and expands your horizons.

Go dancing. Just like physical activity, dancing can alleviate stress, and it contributes to greater well-being. Hit a club with friends or just crank up some tunes in your living room and dance it out.

Get out in nature. It is true that nature has a way to make you feel calmer and more relaxed. It is also quiet and allows you to engage in self-reflection. A quick walk or hike is a good place to start.

Learn how to meditate. Even just five minutes of meditation per day can help to keep you grounded and it makes it easier to deal with stressors.

Start a journal to keep track of your thoughts and feelings.

Eliminate the clutter in your living space. When your home is more organized and clean, this helps to make you calmer. Clutter naturally induces feelings of stress.

Make sure to get adequate sleep. Get yourself on a regular sleeping schedule and stick to it. If you want to take a nap during the day, keep it to an hour or less so that it does not interfere with your ability to sleep at night.

Conclusion

Narcissism can only be defused by stepping back and stepping on your ego. You have the power to change who you are to a positive light. Ask yourself who you want to be and what you like to do. Stick to it like it is your dream. The first step to reach it is to acquire a psychologically healthy personality. With the help of mental health professionals, you can unleash your capabilities as an individual, and soon enough, you will have the undying power to reach your timely success and happiness.

It will not be easy in the beginning. But with passion, time, courage, and determination, you can get out of the prison of your own mind. There is always a way back to your real self. Start by asking for medical help. Once you can overcome your narcissistic personality, you will finally be able to get the genuine love and happiness you want. It may take time and constant effort, but never give up no matter how tiring it gets. After all, the best person that can help you get out of your unhealthy situation is yourself. You exist with a purpose, with the help of psychological intervention, everything will fall into place. All you need is to have faith in yourself and on the process.

Key Points: There will always be a need for psychological evaluation and intervention. People will not be innovated such process if there is no need for it. Psychological help is not only for people with disorders or psychosis. It is time to break the stigma in your society that psychological help is for all people who want to get over their self-defeating tendencies and have a more definite goal in life.

Call to Action: Do not be ashamed when people only you out of seeking psychological help. It is not them you are trying to fix, but your own thinking. Instead of ruminating on those negative feelings, voice them out to people nicely. Make them understand that psychological help will heal you from your mental and psychological malfunctions. So, when you get out of there, it will be like a brand new you - better, more likable, and bolder to achieve your dreams someday.